Education of Muslim Girls

Role of Stakeholders

Dr. Nabila Qureshi

BLUEROSE PUBLISHERS
India | U.K.

Copyright © Dr. Nabila Qureshi 2023

All rights reserved by author. No part of this publication may be reproduced, stored in a retrieval system or transmitted in any form or by any means, electronic, mechanical, photocopying, recording or otherwise, without the prior permission of the author. Although every precaution has been taken to verify the accuracy of the information contained herein, the publisher assumes no responsibility for any errors or omissions. No liability is assumed for damages that may result from the use of information contained within.

BlueRose Publishers takes no responsibility for any damages, losses, or liabilities that may arise from the use or misuse of the information, products, or services provided in this publication.

For permissions requests or inquiries regarding this publication, please contact:

BLUEROSE PUBLISHERS
www.BlueRoseONE.com
info@bluerosepublishers.com
+91 8882 898 898
+4407342408967

ISBN: 978-93-5819-416-6

Cover design: Shivam
Typesetting: Namrata Saini

First Edition: November 2023

ABSTRACT

Education is perceived as a tool for liberation among the common people. It is through the medium of education people comprehend their substantial situations and surrounding and make conscious effort for the improvement, which enables them to prepare to confront the social, political and cultural issues suitably. Hence each citizen of the nation, irrespective of the gender, caste, religion, race have a right to be educated. According to the statistical data of Census 2011, AISHE report (2018-19), the rate of higher education among Muslims in India is less than the other socio- religious communities residing in the country.

The contemporary research work is descriptive research taken up with the objective to study; Numbers of Muslim girls enrolled in secondary and higher secondary classes in and around Vadodara city, to explore the roles of the stakeholder associated in the education of Muslim girls, to understand the home environment of Muslim girls and to find out the career aspiration of Muslim girls.

Stratified random sampling was used, to collect data from 542 participants comprising of Muslim girls studying in XI and XII standard of Muslim Managed schools, higher secondary school teachers, principal, and parents of the Muslim girls. Tools used in the study were questionnaire and interview schedule by visiting schools and doing home visits. Collected data was analyzed using correlation and ANOVA, and data on open ended questions was analyzed using content analysis.

The findings of the study highlight the ratio of Muslim girls pursuing higher education is still very less, as they drop-out from higher secondary classes because of various socio-economic and cultural factors. The study also explores the role of the stakeholders associated towards higher education among Muslim girls and provide suggestions with a view to improve the existing higher educational scenario of Muslim girls within the city, to bring about a positive change by affirmative actions and deliberations.

Key Words: Role of stakeholders, Management of Muslim managed schools, Career aspirations of Muslim girls, Higher secondary education, home environment.

ACKNOWLEDGEMENT

The world of academic is a better place, thanks are expressed to all those who want others to develop in the field of academics. Thanks are expressed to all those who have been a pillar in the life journey, in shaping me, what I am today.

First of all, I earnestly express my gratitude to my research co-guide, **Dr. Anitha Thomas**, who has helped me in identifying the relevant study topic and for her constant motivation. She stood beside me as a strong pillar, supporting, making me learn new things, relearn and unlearn the required things. Expressing gratitude from the bottom of my heart for all the support that she has extended to me.

Expressing thanks to my guide, **Dr. Archana Tomar,** for facilitating all the requirements of the doctoral work according to the university norms.

My Parents deserved a heartful of thanks for their never-ending support, encouragement, and always blessed me with good wishes, to attain success in life. Gratitude to my better half, **Kamil Raza** for his constant support and motivation to make use of best of my academic abilities and standing beside me for any help needed as well as ensuring to take care of my sweet daughter **Kashaf**. Both my sisters **Zeba and Tanveer**, deserves gratitude for always supporting in my decisions.

Kashaf deserves a big thank you for always being a polite and not very demanding child since she was 2 years old. Mumma loves you very Much!

Gratitude to all my other family members, teachers, colleagues, friends for rendering the direct and indirect support. Thanks to all the principals of the school who have permitted me to conduct the study and gather data from the staff as well as from the students as well as facilitating interaction with the parents.

The Almighty can never be thanks for all his blessings and all the best things laid for me in my destiny.

Dr. Nabila Qureshi

CONTENTS

Chapter-I: Conceptual Framework 1

1.0 Introduction 3
1.1 Educational Status of Muslims in India 6
1.2.0 Educational Status of Females in other Countries 12
1.2.1 Educational Status of Muslim Women in India ... 13
1.2.2 Educational Status of Muslims in Gujarat 15
1.3 Historical Foundation of Muslim Women's
Education in India 17
1.4 Government Intiatives for the Educational
Upliftment of the Muslim.. 18
1.4.1 Programmes and Policies for the Educational
Upliftment of the Minority Community in India 18
1.5 Muslim Women and Employment 20
1.5.1 Role of Education in Human Development 21
1.5.2 Human Relation Theory and Education 23
1.5.3 Human Capital Theory and Education 24
1.5.4 Stakeholder Theory and Education 25
1.5.5 The Concept and The Role of the Stakeholders ... 26
1.6 Types of School 28
1.7 Research Questions: 34
1.8 Ethical Consideration in the Study: 35

Chapter-II: Review of Literature 37

2.0 Introduction 38
2.1 Studies Related to Muslim Girls' Education........... 38
2.2 Studies Related to Gender Equality and
Empowerment 46
2.3 Studies Related to Islamic Perspectives on

Education of Women 51
2.4 Studies Related to the Stakeholders in the
Educational Institutions 54
2.4.1 School as an Educational Stakeholder 54
2.4.1 A) Studies Related to Infrastructural
Development InSchools 55
2.4.1 B) Studies Related to the Teaching Quality,
ProfessionalDevelopment Opportunities, Incentives
of Teachers 58
2.4.1 C) Studies Related to the Academic, Social and
Psychological Development of Students 60
Overview of the Studies Related to Schools an
Educational Stakeholders 63
2.4.2 Parents as an Educational Stakeholders 64
2.4.2 A) Studies Related to Socio-Economic Status
of Parents 64
2.4.1 B) Studies Related to Educational Status
of Parents 67
2.4.2 C) Studies Related to Occupational Status of
Parents 70
2.4.2 D) Studies Related To The Involvement of
Parents and theFamily Structure 72
2.4.3 Community as an Educational Stakeholder 74
2.4.4 Government as an Educational Stakeholder 76
2.5 Rationale of the Study 83
2.6 Implications for the Study 84

Chapter-III: Research Methodology 89

3.0 Statement of the Study 90
3.1 Objectives of the Study 90
3.2 Explanation of the Terms 91
3.3 Study Variables 92

3.4 Research Design 92
3.5 Universe of the Study 92
3.6 Selection of Sample from total Population and
Sample Size 93
3.7 Overview of the Total Sampling 95
3.8 Tools Used for Data Collection 95
3.9 Tool Creation 97
3.10 Tool Validation 98
3.11 Source of Data Collection 99
3.12 Process of Data Collection 100
3.13 Problems Faced During Data Collection 102
3.14 Data Analysis 102
3.15 De Limitation of the Study 103
3.16 Limitation of the Study 103

Findings, Conclusions and Suggestions 105

5.4 Major Findings: This Section of the chapter
describes the major findings of the study as: 136
5.4.1 Section-A) Findings related to the study
background: 136
5.4.2 Section-B) - Findings related to the elementary
information of the study: Objective: 1 a) To study
the number of Muslim girls in secondary and higher
secondary classes in and around Vadodara 138
5.4.3 Section-C)- Findings related to the Direct
Impact of Schools towards the education of
Muslim girls: 139
5.4.4 (Section-C)- Findings related to the Direct
Impact of Schools towards the educationof
Muslim girls 140
5.4.5 Objective 3: To study the home environment
of Muslim girls 142

5.4.6 (Section-C)- Findings related to the Direct Impact of Schools towards the education of Muslim girls 143

5.4.7 (Section-D)- Findings related to the Indirect Impact of community and government towards the education of Muslim girls. 144

5.5 Discussions of Results: 145

5.6 Conclusions of the Study: 146

5.7 Suggestions from the Study: 147

5.8 Summary table of the Suggestions 151

5.9 Explanation of the Theoretical Frame Work 153

5.10 Scope of Further Research 154

References 155

Books 156

CHAPTER-I

Conceptual Framework

General idea of the Chapter

This chapter outline the origin of the research idea, on the title "Role of Stakeholders towards the Education of Muslim girls in and around Vadodara City", which explains the importance of education in this competitive era. As this era is marked by increase in technological advancement, increase in job competition, there is a need for development among all the socio- religious communities within the nation, which can be gained through the medium of education. It is with the overall development of all the socio religious communities, the inclusive development of the nation shall happen. The filaments of the chapter are weaved from the literacy data of Census 2011, which represents the lower education among Muslim community, and specifically the Muslim females in our country, and in the state of Gujarat, that overlays the way paves the way for developing the objectiveof the study:

> 1. To study the numbers of Muslim girls enrolled in secondary and higher secondary classes in and around Vadodara city

The chapter further elaborates on the foremost explanations for the lower educational statusof Muslim women in the country in comparison with other countries and also focusses on the historical progress of educational development of Muslim women in our country. The chapter also tries to bring out the linkages between the various management theories such as human development, human capital, human relation and the stakeholder's theory in relation with the education, and also discusses the inventiveness of the Indian government to increase the educational status among Muslims and especially Muslim females, which lays the origin of the research questions.

1. Who are the stakeholders associated with the education Muslim girls?
2. What are the roles stakeholders play in influencing education of Muslim girls?

1.0 INTRODUCTION

"Education is the great engine of personal development. It is through education that the daughter of a peasant can become a doctor, that the son of a mineworker can become the head of the mine, that a child of farmworkers can become the president of a great nation. Itis what we make out of what we have, not what we are given, that separates one person from another". - Nelson Mandela

The present 21st century era, is the utmost advanced passé of social evolution, in which, knowledge, communiqué, association, dexterity, completely remains astonishing. Education, over its diverse structures, partakes imperative part through numerous dissimilar resources. Education is measured as the solitarily greatest substantial resources resulting in social as well as economic development. Group of people through decent acquaintance, and skills will lead to inclusive advancement of the nation. **Bano (2017).** Thus, it is essential that all the citizens of the nation from all the sections of the society, irrespective of their caste, class, religion and gender should be well educated and well trained.

It is in this context; the education of women is very important and a crucial range of concernsfor policymakers. Seeing the data on the educational advancement of women in India, the data of NITI Aayog literacy rate for females demonstrates at 65.46%, whereas, it shows to 82.14% for males in 2011 in India, which displays subordinate level of literateness among Indian females.

Congruently, the statistics for the state of Gujarat as per **Census 2011,** shows female literacy rate at 70.73%, and Male literacy rate at 87.23%. Thus, both the national as well as the statewise literacy information reveals the inferior literacy rates among females. However, it is imperative to understand Management of Education. It has a hierarchy from, national level to state level and local urban bodies as well as rural bodies and socio-religious organization providing education.

Educational Management

The concept of Educational Management is a systematic process of planning, organizing, directing and controlling the events of an educational institution through optimum utilization of manpower (Children, teachers, Parents, employees, university /boards of education, office bodies at local, state and at central level) and the substantial resources (Infrastructural resources, finance) with an intention to successfully and resourcefully achieve purposes of teaching, and need based research and extension work. At the central level, the Ministry of Human Resource Development is the apex body, accountable for all matters relating to education, comprising of inclusive preparation of programmes and disseminating supervision and guidance for further implementation. The central government has formed specialized institutions and organizations to aid and advise government in formulation and implementation of various policies and programmes. The few apex institutions or boards are enlisted as under:

1. Central Advisory Board of Education (CABE)

2. National Council of Education Research and Training (NCERT)
3. University Grants Commission (UGC)
4. Council of Scientific and Industrial Research (CSIR)
5. All India Council for Technical Education (AICTE)
6. Distance Education Council (DEC)
7. Association of Indian Universities (AIU)
8. National University of Educational Planning and Administration (NUEPA)

Different bodies at the State level, are:

1. Department of Education
2. State Council for Educational Research and Training (SCERT)
3. District Primary Education Programme (DPEP)
4. Regional or Circle level Bodies
5. District Level Bodies
6. Block Level Bodies
7. State Higher Education Commission
8. State Institute of Educational Management and Training (SIEMAT)
9. State Institute of Educational Technology (SIET)

Thus, it can be said Ministry of Human Resource development in India, state level as well as the local level bodies plays a very significant role in educational management in the country. Hence with the help of the strategic and statutory bodies enacted at central, state and local level and moreover, with the intention to bring out comprehensive education, it is necessary to have educational access and progress of both males and females, belonging toall the socio- religious communities. The National Minority Commission in India has described Muslims on the basis of faith as one of the largest minority groups among other minorities such as Christians, Sikhs, Buddhists and Jains.

1.1 EDUCATIONAL STATUS OF MUSLIMS IN INDIA

The primary marginal community in India facets enlightening backwardness in contrast with other socio-religious groups within the nation. In 2005 the United Progressive Alliance government, noting the lack of accurate knowledge on Indian Muslims' social, legal, and educational status, commissioned a report on the thirteen states with the largest Muslim populations. The report was to query into issues such as infant and maternal mortality rates,access to education and drop-out rates, health status, employment, and access to bank credit, led by Justice Rajinder Sachar, the report found that "the Indian Muslim community exhibitsdeficits and deprivation in practically all dimensions of development" **(Sachar 2006).** It recommended mechanisms to guarantee, freedom of opportunities for Indian Muslims.

The facts and figures on the literacy level of the Indian Muslim community as revealed by the **(Census data 2011)** is given below

Table- 1.1 Literacy rate of Socio- religious communities as per Census 2011

Religion	Literacy Rate (Total)	Literacy Rate (Males)	Literacy Rate (Females)
Hindus	65.1	76.2	53.2
Muslims	59.1	67.6	50.1
Christians	80.3	84.4	76.2
Sikhs	69.4	75.2	63.1
Buddhists	72.7	83.1	61.7
Jains	94.1	97.4	90.6
Other religions	47.0	60.8	33.2
India	64.8	75.3	53.7

Source: Census 2011

From the census data, literacy rates among Muslims are much lower than the literacy rate of other socio- religious communities within the nation.

In addition to the Census data 2011, the data revealed by **All India Survey on Higher Education (AISHE)**, undertaken by the Ministry of Human Resource and Development, Government of India depicts the representation of Muslim community is much lower than that of those belonging to the Scheduled Caste and Scheduled Tribes residing in India, whichis relevant from the following table:

Table: 1.2 Enrollment of Muslim students in Higher Education

Year	Muslim%	ST %	SC %	OBC %
2010-11	3.8	4.4	11.1	27.6
2011-12	3.9	4.5	12.2	30.1
2012-13	4.2	4.4	12.8	31.2
2013-14	4.3	4.6	13.1	32.4
2014-15	4.5	4.8	13.4	32.8
2015-16	4.7	4.9	13.9	33.75
2016-17	4.9	5.1	14.2	34.4
2017-18	5.0	5.2	14.4	35.0
2018-19	5.2	5.5	14.9	

Source AISHE report (2018-19)

The above data of AISHE report, (conducted by MHRD, GOI) clearly indicates that there is arise in the growth rate of education among Muslim community, from the calendar year 2010-11 to 2018-19, yet the enrolment in higher education is much lower than the scheduled and other backward communities of the country.

Thus, it can be said that Indian Muslims make up more than 12% of the Indian population, which is very high on any account, and in terms of actual figures, the numbers were estimated to 17.22 crores according to All India Religion Census data 2011. Therefore, their economic and educational growth is very important for the country's progress. No nation will boast of growth if its large minority lags behind and its large majority remains illiterate and poor. **Engineer (2002).**

From the above data and evidences of various reports, it can be said that the educational status among Indian Muslims is really a matter of concern **(Abdullah 2020)**. Identifying various reasons for the lower educational status among Muslim community, it can be said that the major factors for lower educational status are less preference towards the education; due to religious restrictions (which Quran do not impose), lack of awareness on importance of education, and prevalence of socio- economic factors among Indian Muslims. As a corrective measure, the educationistand the other activist from the community have understood the grave problem of lower education among Muslim community and the measures are also undertaken such as establishing the schools and Madrassa to improve the educational status of the community. The ministry has also encouraged establishment of educational institutions for the educational progress of the community with a view to realize the full potential of India's human capital, with fairness and excellence. "All minorities...shall have the right to establish and administer education institutions of their own" is the mandate, provided underArticle 30(1) of the Constitution. Government is committed to address the current backwardness of minorities' education, especially Muslims, which is the large chunk of minorities.

Another dominating reason for the lower educational progress of Muslim community is thecommunity people do not foresee the education converting in to formal employment, thus this is also one of the reasons the Muslim parents do not invest in the education of children forboth girls and boys. Similarly, for the girl child, the girls are not allowed for higher educationfor various reasons like early marriages, purdah system, lack of safety etc., and young girls are burdened with household responsibilities and siblings care, ultimately, they drop out from their education. Thus because of such beliefs and perceptions, the representation of Muslims is less in formal employment both in private as well as in public sectors. (**Abdullah2020**)

Another significant reason is focus of giving "Madrassa" education to children, "Madrassa"is the Islamic learning center, which teaches children to recite the Holy Quran and to followthe Islamic principles of performing prayers five times a day, teaching prophetic ideologies.Thus, 'Madrassa' does not impart the contemporary education.

In present context, as well, the Muslim women, are always under discussions in numerous academic, research and policy making forums on the issues, such as purdah system, polygamy and All India Personal law board. Yet, it is a tragedy that there are several customsand practices in Islamic societies, actually ignored, misinterpreted or are denied on the rightsgiven to women by Islam as a religion.

Focusing on the educational attainment and participation in labor force of Muslim women,no Quranic citation as well as the preaching's imposed any restrictions. Studying the Quranic narration, it can be said that in this regard, the verses exemplify the youngest wife of the Prophet, Hazrat Aaaisha, who was a great Islamic scholar and had taught number of eminent scholars at that time. she was also known for encouraging women to educate themselves and to others and explaining them the importance of education in Islam.

Likewise, the Quranic excerpts also narrates that a Muslim woman has all the rights to earn money as well. And exemplifying, the verses cite the example of the Prophet's wife Khadijah- who was a successful business trader and the Prophet himself was very happy when he was employed by Khadijah and later on, he encouraged her for future success. Thus, the verses and the archetypal citations of the Quran, clearly mentions the importance of education and also gives liberty to the Women folk to enter the labour force.

In accordance with the Quranic excerpt, **Shazli and Asma (2015)** writes that Islam puts a greater importance on education by quoting its philosophy which says that "go in quest of knowledge to as distant as a place as China", thus there is no religious restrictions that obstructs the educational progress. In terms of gender equality in gaining education, **Fauzia(2017)** writes that according to Islam there is no discrimination between genders in terms of acquiring education, in- fact it provides equality of seeking knowledge and learning for both the genders.

Thus, on the basis of the discussions and citations on the beliefs, practices, prevalent amongMuslim community, it can be said that there are lot of misinterpretations pertaining to the beliefs, practices, the customs followed by the Muslim community, which is because of lower education and correct and authentic knowledge among the Muslim community, specifically the females of the community. Inadequate knowledge is always a hindrance in the socio-economic progress of Muslim girls and women.

Hence, the education of Muslim girls is a serious issue, the access of education among the girls will bring about the social, economic development not only within the family or the community but will also improve in the national progress, as this will also increase the literacy level among the Muslim population- as one educated woman in the family will bringchanges in the whole life of the family and for the coming generations as well.

1.2.0 EDUCATIONAL STATUS OF FEMALES IN OTHER COUNTRIES

Attaining education is one of the basic fundamental rights of every individual, according to Islam religion does not impose any restrictions on Muslim females for attaining education andentering the labour market, however, there are gender inequalities noticed with reference to women's education both in developing and developed countries. And specifically, the educational status of Muslim women is a debatable issue since a decade across the globe.

Drawing to the history, in the beginning of 20th century, Muslim women were left out from various areas like politics, social, as majority of the them were illiterate. **AK (2019).** According to (**Zengenene and Susanti, 2019**) women are constantly repressed in all the facets like education, participation in work force and politics. Furthermore, internationally also, women in the 21st century still are unable to earn the strong base as compared to the men especially in the Muslim nations, and they are illtreated due to the socio-cultural backgroundand the prevalence of the patriarchal system within the family and the society at large. **(Haque, Sarker, Rahman and Rakibuddin, 2020).**

Contrary to the above studies, the study conducted by **Mcclendon, David and Hackett, Conrad and Potančoková, Michaela and Stonawski, Marcin and Skirbekk, Vegard". (2018)** shows interesting finding, which says that "the educational attainment of Muslim women is noticed in the progressive form in the Middle East and North Africa". The educational level among Muslim women has also been noticed in a progressive way in countries like Egypt, Tunisia, Israel and Iran.

According to the study done by (**Haque, Muhammad, et al (2020),** 70% of the Muslim women receive education in Middle East and North Africa, more than 90% of women are educated in Indonesia and Malaysia, 40% Muslim women are educated in Pakistan and Bangladesh has shown a gradual increase from 50- 70% after 2010.

1.2.1 EDUCATIONAL STATUS OF MUSLIM WOMEN IN INDIA

Considering the plight of Muslim women, historically the women from the Muslim communities were not allowed to go outside their homes, they were not sent to gain education, they had to believe and follow the purdah system. Muslim girl child was labelled as "Choola, Chadar and Chardeewari" according to the report of committee of Governors on the welfare of minorities, in the year 1977. This report shows the high level of illiteracy among the Muslim.

women as the cause of lower status of Muslim women in the community. The dominance of the impact of patriarchal structure on the education of Muslim girls, is mentioned by **Hasan and Menon (2004)** that Muslim women are not involved in India's social, economic, or political progressions because of patriarchal norms in All India Muslim personal law board. Poverty and patriarchy particularly impact Muslim women's education. Wherein, girls are educated to an optimal level to find a suitable marriage partner with relatively higher levels of education (Muslim male literacy rates are also low in comparison with other socio- religious communities), and a belief that investing in a girl's education brings little returns to the family.

Ahmed and Mistry (2010) said that Muslim women are conscious of the importance of education and aim to be educated, to make choices, to have their voices heard in the choices they make, and to partake in decision making in family matters. However, poverty and absence of information about financial motivations for women's education endure to hold women's position.

According to **(Census data 2011)** only 50% of Muslim women are literate. The literacy rate of Muslim women is 17.5% points lower than the male literacy rate and 3.6% lower than the national average of female literacy rates. According to the **(AISHE 2018-19)** survey on the enrolment of students in higher education, 5.23% are from the Muslim community and 2.32% belong to the other minority communities. The data also reveals that among Muslim minority number of male students is higher than the female students in higher education. (Detail description of the data is shown in following table 1.3)

Table:1.3 Gender wise enrolment of Muslim students in Higher Education

Particulars	Male (%)	Female (%)
Enrolment of students from Muslim community	50.7	49.29
Enrolment of students from other communities	45.74	54.25

(Source: AISHE Report 2018-19)

The above facts and figures, and previous studies it can be inferred that the educational status of Muslim women in Indian context, is lower in terms of both the overall literacy rate and also the number of Muslim females is less in higher education as well.

1.2.2 EDUCATIONAL STATUS OF MUSLIMS IN GUJARAT

As per the report of the Sachar committee- the committee formed to investigate the socio- economic condition of Gujarat's Muslim in the parliament in 2016, the committee shows the literacy rate among Muslims in Gujarat to 73.5%, in comparison with the national average of 59.1%. The data on the educational attainment of Muslims in Gujarat is also representing a positive picture of Gujarat Muslims. (Detail description is shown Figure-1.0and Figure -1.1)

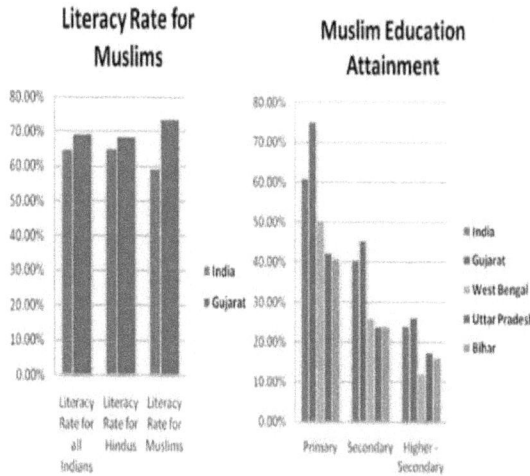

Fig- 1.0 and Fig-1.1(Source: Sachar Committee Report)

- The data in Fig1.0 shows that the literacy rate among Muslims in Gujarat is 5pointshigher than the Hindus i.e., 73.5 % for Muslims and 68.3% for Hindus.

- The educational attainment of Muslims at primary stage as shown in Figure- 4is 74.9%compared to the national average of 60.9%

- Figure-1.1 depicts the 45.3% of educational attainment at secondary stage, better tanthe national average of 40.5%
- The data in the Figure-1.1 shows the data at higher secondary education level at 26.1%for Muslims, which is again ahead of national average of 23.9%.

Thus, from the above facts and figures pertaining to the educational status of Muslims in the state of Gujarat, it can be said that the Muslims are in a better situation in the state.

All the above data, reveals a progressive development of Gujarat's Muslims in education sector, however, the educational status specifically of Muslim women in the state is less, which is evident from Figure-3, demonstrating the literacy level in the state. The data showsthat literacy among Muslim women is less as compared to Muslim men. The enrolment of the Muslim females in the higher education is less in number, which is evident from the AISHE report of 2018-19.

Table:1.4 Gender wise enrollment of students in Higher Education for Gujarat State

Particulars	Male (%)	Female (%)
Enrolment of students fromMuslim community	56.24	43.75
Enrolment of students fromother communities	53.95	46.04

(Source: AISHE Report 2018-19)

The enrolment of Muslim male students in higher education is 56.24% which is higher than2.29% than the enrolment of students from other communities, whereas for females it is 43.75%, which is less than 2.29% than those from other communities. The enrolment of Muslim males is 12.49% higher than the Muslim females in higher education. Hence, with the help of the data, it can be said that though the education level among Muslims from Gujarat region is showing a positive picture, yet the data shows that the education of females is less and the issue of the educational status of Muslim women in the country is a significant matter.

1.3 HISTORICAL FOUNDATION OF MUSLIM WOMEN'S EDUCATION IN INDIA

Drawing to the historical foundation of education among Muslim women, the education of females was rarely focused on. The area of the education of Muslim women was primary elevated at the "All-Male Muslim Educational Congress" held in 1896. Subsequently, in 1906, "Sheikh Abdullah and his wife Wahid Jahan Begum" laid the foundation of a separateschool for girls at Aligarh. "Purdah nashin Madrasa" a separate school for girls was established in Kolkata, in 1913. Followed by, in the year 1914 Begum of Bhopal, Sultan Jahan Begum established lot of educational institutions in Bhopal and recognized free and compulsory primary education in the year 1918. Similarly, during 19th century the writings of BegumRokaiya through her various articles and books, had played a significant role in hovering the status and constructing identity of Muslim women. Thus, it can be said the issue of Muslim women's education is of greater concern since 19th century, however in India, the educational status of Muslim women continues to be a concern.

1.4 GOVERNMENT INTIATIVES FOR THE EDUCATIONAL UPLIFTMENT OFTHE MUSLIM.

School education, including primary, intermediate and higher secondary education, which is either general or professional education, and vocational education, is part of the Indian education system. The Ministry of Human Resource Development primarily oversees the Indian education system (MHRD). The related bodies at the central level are the National Council for Educational Research and Training (NCERT), the University Grants Commission(UGC), the All-India Council for Technical Education (AICTE) and the National Council for Teacher Education (NCTE), and the Department of Education and the State Council for Educational Research and Training (SCERT).

1.4.1 PROGRAMMES AND POLICIES FOR THE EDUCATIONAL UPLIFTMENT OF THE MINORITY COMMUNITY IN INDIA

For the purpose of upliftment of minorities, there are various programmes and policies, established for the educational improvement of the minority community listed below:

a. INFRASTRUCTURE DEVELOPMENT IN MINORITY INSTITUTIONS (IDMI)

IDMI has been established to enhance infrastructure in private aided/unaided minority schools/institutions in order to enhance quality of education to minority children. The relevant features of IDMI scheme are: - i) The scheme would facilitate education of minorities by expanding and establishing school infrastructure in Minority Institutions in order to expand facilities for formal education to children of minority communities. ii) The scheme will cover the entire country but, preference will be given to minority institutions (private aided / unaided schools) located in districts, blocks and towns having a minority population above 20%. iii) The scheme will, encourage educational facilities for girls, children with special needs and those who are most deprived of educational facilities.

b. PRE - MATRIC SCHOLARSHIP SCHEME:

The scholarship provided for students from minority communities at pre- matric. The scholarship would promote and inspire parents from minority groups to send their school- going children to school, reduce their school education financial costs and assist their attempts to help their children complete their school education.

c. MERIT CUM MEANS SCHOLARSHIP

The Minority Scholarship is a scholarship structure initiated by the central government for increasing the education proportion in minority community students. Under the Ministry of Minority Affairs – MOMA Scholarship Scheme: "students belonging to **Muslim, Sikh, Christian, Buddhist, Jain and Parsi** minority communities can benefit by the Merit-Cum-Means Scholarship 2020-21 for vocational and technical courses". **The beneficiary of these National Minority Scholarships receives a scholarship amount of up to Rs. 20,000 per year, at undergraduate and post graduate levels.**

d. MAULANA AZAD NATIONAL FELLOWSHIP SCHEME

"Maulana Azad National Fellowship scheme" is the scheme which is operated by Ministry of Human Resource Development through University Grants Commission as the nodal agency, with an objective to provide five-year fellowship by giving financial help to students from the minority community aspiring to undertake research studies awarding them the degree of M.Phil. or Ph.D.

The government has enacted and implemented various policies and programmes for the educational upliftment of minority community from time to time. The government has also taken due consideration of women folk of the country and specifically for women belonging to minority community. Following are few studies depicting the scenario of Muslim women and their participation in employment sector.

1.5 MUSLIM WOMEN AND EMPLOYMENT

It is evident from the above-mentioned studies and data that there is lower educational progress of Muslim women, irrespective of the its basis since 19th century and the governmental initiatives for the upliftment of the community. Because of lack of education, there is lack of involvement and representation of Muslim women in the employment sector as well, sixty percent of Muslim women are self-employed in comparison with other socio-religious communities of India **Kazi (1999)**. Muslim women are prodigiously entrepreneurial (in homebased work) like sewing, embroidery, zariwork, chikan jobs, ready-made clothes, agarbatti rolling, beedi rolling, etc., and their working conditions are characterized by low pay, bad working conditions, lack of toilet, crèche facilities, and absence of social security. **Lakshmi Devi (2014)** The major reasons for the lower educational accomplishment and employment, are the restrictions imposed on Muslim women and girls pertaining to their mobility outside their homes, the patriarchal family structure, preference of education towards their sons rather than their daughters, and giving preference to religious education through Madrassa only for the daughters. **Sacchar report(2006).** Hence it can be inferred that there is a need to bring empowerment among the Muslim women which can be brought in through the medium of education only, as education puts emphasis on the development of an individual, which is substantially dependent on the "Human and their environment". Therefore, it is imperative to focus on and find out what type of environment leads to development of Human and in what way? Moreover, in order to bring out overall development of an individual, it is essential to invest or to create the resources (investing in human capital), which are required to bring about the development in totality comprising of Human Development, Human Relation, Human Capital and the support of stakeholders in the educational institutions.

1.5.1 ROLE OF EDUCATION IN HUMAN DEVELOPMENT

The era of 1990's, marked the recognition of the concept of human development generally, and thus numerous programmes like Earth Summit (1992), Education for All (1990 and 2000), "Millennium Development Goals (2000)", "Sustainable Development Goals (2015)" has played a larger attention on education. "Human development" is one of the recognized and valued method to measure, describe and direct the changing development process globally. **Haq (2000)** contends human development, "a development paradigm that is about much more than the rise or fall of national income. It is about generating an environment in which people can develop their full potential and lead productive, creative life in accord with their needs and interests". The definition focus on constructing the environment, wherein people have access to the available resources and to make every human being, an independent being so that one can satisfy their needs.

In order to meet the new challenges, education has become the demand for the nation, because of new development in science, innovations as well as changes in to the employment sector as well. Along with meeting the new contests, education is also neededto resolve many social issues, which has also been emphasized by Human Development Report (2000) by stating that "education is very helpful in tackling many social problems and bring about empowerment, especially to the females".

Resting importance of education and human development, UNESCO, also states that education is primary change agent for "human development". In order to bring change in asociety, social development also plays a dominating role, thus to make transformation socially, it is imperative to have good educational institutions, in the same line Patnaik **(1995),** in his article "The international Context and the 'Kerala Model'", says that any social development needs a group of intellectuals for its smooth functioning and it is the responsibility of the educational institutions to produce such intellectuals. Moreover, education will not only produce the intellectuals, rather it will also help in developing social,cultural, political, and economic system.

For the needed transformation it is required to have a joint support of all those who are a part of the social system, stressing on the same point **Reed (2008)**, using the term 'ordinarycitizen', in his book "Human Development and social power: Perspectives from South Asia", says that through education even the ordinary citizen, will be able to organize and mobilize social and political influences, in order to develop healthy and lively society.

Along with making changes in the social environment, it is also essential to bring variations in the economic system as well, so as to have an improved living standard among the citizens, **Chauhan V (2016)** in his paper "Conceptualizing Education in the Human Development Paradigm" by mentioning that it is not only the education, which is sufficient for an individual to live a dignified life, but simultaneously along with good education, a good 'work' is also necessary. **Human Development Report (2015)** also mentions that there is a common relationship between work and the human development, the report states that, it is the work that reinforces its relation with human development, it is the work which not only gives a decent standard of living to an individual, but it also aids in solving social problems like poverty, unemployment, gender inequality, solidarity.

Hence, it can be concluded that education is an essential requirement in this 21st century, it is the education which fosters, a positive socio- cultural environment, positive political and economic environment, and also governs the wellbeing and income of not only the individuals, but groups.

1.5.2 HUMAN RELATION THEORY AND EDUCATION

The writings of the **Mary Parker Follet (1933),** who was also known as 'Prophet of Management', has emphasized that no individual can become complete individual unless one is associated with any of the group. She further says that it is very much important to have a consistent and interactive relationship among the members of the group. In an educational institution, in reference to human relation approach, the status of all individuals associated with the system, particularly their opinions, desires and biases governs the system. Exemplifying the same, the requirement of the school and the teachers are corresponding, both require each other for balancing to attain optimum results.

Thus, the major focus of the human relation school of thought is to consider the needs and goals of every individual and to provide the developmental opportunities to them so that theindividual can accomplish their own goals and attainments.

1.5.3 HUMAN CAPITAL THEORY AND EDUCATION

The beginning of the Human Capital Theory lies in the article which was written by T.W Schultz (1961). The main idea of the theory is to make investments in 'human resources' with an aim to improve their productivity and therefore concurrently to improve their earnings. The fundamental postulation states that that proper education is very much contributory to progress or to bring improvement in the productive capacity of a given population. Wood Hall (1997) writes that through proper education, an investment is madein 'human capital', which is valuable than the 'physical capital'. Since the era of 1960's, the"Human capital theory' is the most significant and persuasive theory in western countries, as many countries has established their government and educational policies by using the human capital theory as their base.

Babalola (2003) has presented his ideas on investments in human capital by giving following opinions:

a. The upcoming/current generation needs to be provided with the appropriate information, and facts which is gathered by earlier generation.
b. The upcoming/current generation should be educated and trained on how prevailing knowledge could be used to bring innovations in various manufacturing approaches andeven in social services.
c. The generation must be stimulated to develop completely novel thoughts, products, procedures, and approaches through innovative ways.

According to the views of **Fagerlind and Saha (1997)** the natural resources that country owns and the capital power are inactive factors, whereas its human are the dynamic and lively resources who develops the country's social, economic and political organizations and further contributes to the development of the nation as a whole. Thus, from the above- mentioned viewpoints it can be said that the that proper education will be beneficial in accomplishing the positive results is been stressed by various scholar of the time. It is through proper education only, the appropriate knowledge can be acquired, and especially with reference to Indian context, which comprises of population following multilinguistic cultures, it is the proper education that can bring out people from the conservative, orthodox, superstitious beliefs and practices, prevalent in the society and generate healthy and positivenvironment for all its citizens. Thus, it is very much essential for each and every resident of the country and it is the fundamental right of every voter to get proper education.

1.5.4 STAKEHOLDER THEORY AND EDUCATION

Freeman's (1984) work is considered as pivotal work in developing stakeholder theory. The author points out that for the effective management of any organization, it needs a change model. Not only this, but it is also very imperative to manage the relationship between the stakeholders, to achieve the organizational objectives/ goals **(Freeman et al., 2020)**

The era of modern technology, makes obligation on the industries, to develop new and innovative ways in their manufacturing process, in the similar manner, in order to produce the intellectuals, it is imperative for the educational institutions to bring about improvement in the teaching quality, by adopting technological means in teaching learning. There will bean additional collaboration amongst the stakeholders within the organization, if their interestand the work done will bring benefit to them, is the basic assumption of the stakeholder theory. Additionally, the associated stakeholders, through their acquaintance and capabilities will be beneficial for the organization through mutual exchange of thoughts, which will decrease the possibility of disappointment among the groups. **(Esterhuyse, 2019; Ngah and Wong, 2020).** This can be done through proper interaction with the stakeholders, which will also be helpful in dealing with the changing demands of the associated stakeholders (**Li and Nguyen, 2017; Kolding et al., 2018)**

1.5.5 THE CONCEPT AND THE ROLE OF THE STAKEHOLDERS

Stakeholder: "The term stake can be simply described as a share, interest or investment thata certain party attributes to an entity **(Freeman, 1984).** A stakeholder is an individual or group with an interest in the success of an organization in fulfilling its mission—delivering intended results and maintaining the viability of its products, services and outcomes over time" **(Engaging Stakeholders-Sustainability series No-6 2009)**

Based on the system view, the stakeholders involved in the education of Muslim girls can be Internal and external stakeholders.

a) Internal Stakeholders: Internal stakeholders are those individuals who are enrolled with the school system and they are the one who study in the school or perform their duties within the school system, on day-to-day basis and they are the individuals who acquire control over the activities within the school. e.g., the teaching and the non-teaching school staff, the district and the state authorities, the school management boards.

I) School Authorities as Stakeholder: It is the school authorities who are responsible in catering and imparting quality education. It is majorly the school authorities who manage the education for all. For the Study purpose, the attitude of the school authorities including the teaching and the support rendered by the non-teaching staff of the schools towards the education of Muslim girls is looked in to.

External Stakeholders: External stakeholders are those individuals who do not perform their work duties on a daily basis within the school premises, but are associated and gives more attention to the results of the school. They are the individuals who do not acquire control over the activities within the school, but have close association with the school system.

b) I) Parents as Stakeholder: Various associated factors such as awareness, attitude, educational level, income of parents of the Muslim girls are the important factors towards the education of their children. If parents comprehend the importance of education, they will apparently make extensive efforts to give their children the best education. **Ahmed and Mistry (2010)** in their study writes there is "generational change" in the attitudes of the parents who are educated and further expect their children to get good education. The studydeals with exploring the roles and support extended by Muslim parents towards the education of their daughters.

b II) Government as Stakeholder: When it comes in formulating policies, rules and regulations, both for the internal as well as the external stakeholders, the resources, in managing the educational institution, government plays a very pivotal role. The study has also looked into the rules and regulation followed within the school premises and also has focused on the awareness level of both internal as well as external stakeholders pertaining to the support rendered by the government to increase the educational level among the minorities within the country in form of various scholarship programmes laid down for theminorities.

Hence it can be concluded that the efforts of Indian Education system, and consecutive educational policies and programmes have shown considerable outcome in identifying and further connecting the social gaps that restricted the socio- economically disadvantaged population, socio- cultural disadvantaged groups including minorities to have access to quality education.

1.6 TYPES OF SCHOOL

In Indian education system, the schools are managed by different educational agencies as explained diagrammatically

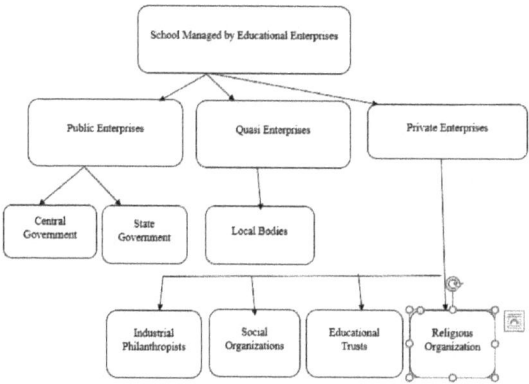

(Fig 1.2 Diagrammatic representation of School managed by educational Enterprises in India

For the purpose of the study, categorization of schools is mentioned below:

Muslim Managed Schools: According to the present study, the Muslim managed schools are those schools, which are managed by Muslim trusts/ organization in Vadodara city andaround.

Government Schools: For the Present study, the schools that are funded, administered, andhave their affiliation with Gujarat Secondary and Higher Secondary Education Board are considered as the government schools.

Private Schools: According to the Study, the schools that manages its fund as well as its administration by the private body, yet follows the rules and regulations of the local and state government and have its affiliation with Gujarat Secondary and Higher Secondary Education Board.

Aided Schools: In context with the present study, the aided educational institute is a privateinstitute that is getting aid from the government of India. And specification related to the qualifications required for appointment as teachers is prescribed by the government in recognized private (both aided and unaided) schools.

The above discussions, on the educational status of Muslim women; the statistical data revealing the lower educational progress of Muslim Community as whole and precisely for the education of Muslim girls gave the derivation of the study objective:

> 1. To Study the number of Muslim girls in secondary and higher secondary classes inand around Vadodara city.
>
> 2. To understand the home environment of the Muslim girls

Having realized, this grave issue, in accordance with the government programmes and schemes levied for the educational progress, there are initiatives taken up by the community stakeholders by establishing the educational institutions, with the intention to increase the educational level, among Muslims and precisely for the girls. This gave the specification ofstratifying the sample of selecting the Schools Managed by Muslim Trust/ bodies, detailed methodology is explained in the successive section.

The study categorizes the schools as one of the important stakeholders in facilitating the education in the community and more specifically for the girls, which gave the insight of formulation of the following research questions:

> 1. What are the views of School Management related to the number ofenrolments of Muslim girls in the higher secondary classes?
>
> 2. How has education influenced the attitude and aspirations of Muslim girls inthe Vadodara district and around?

According to the study done by **Jain (1988)** women folks from the Muslim community in India are considered as a probable substance for the progress of the community. Enhancement of their current status within the community will not only results in the progress of the community, but will also contribute to the national development.

Chaturvedi (2003) says Muslim women are unable to make optimal use of the developmental facilities available to them due to various reasons, hence to improve Muslim women's status, it is imperative to change the community behavior towards the females.

The study conducted by **Shaikh (2013)** brings out the positive aspect of education among Muslim women in the country. The author says that education is a very essential tool to bring about the total development comprising of physical, psychological and spiritual wellbeing for an individual. The study mentions the transformation of parental attitudes among Muslim community, wherein parents strongly want to give their daughters the best education not only with an intention to make them a capable housewife but also with an intention to make them financially independent. The author highlights by saying that the Muslim community also has realized the importance of giving education to the women folk of the community. In the similar line another study undertaken by **Noor (2016)** says that it is a very wrong perception, where people held religious restrictions to be responsible for lower educational status, and also narrates that the private minority organizations and Madrassa are established by the community, to bring improvement in the educational status of the community.

Reviewing available articles, and relating with available literature, it can be said that the status of Indian women from the Muslim community, over a period of time, highlights ongoing low literacy rates and recounts various socio-economic factors like patriarchal family structure, the parental attitude - which holds the belief that investing in girl's education gives no direct result to the family, the minimal contribution of Muslim women in the work force. Correspondingly, all the management theories such as Human development, Human Capital, Stakeholder and Human relation theories also stressed that the education of each and every individual is very much essential for the overall development of the nation, it is true that there are challenges pertaining to the education as a sector, especially for the girlsof the minority community. The collaborative actions with all the associated stakeholders need to be planned so as to make the optimistic changes within the society by imparting quality education to our future generation.

Thus, the contemporary study deals with exploring the roles of the stakeholders and weavedthe process of establishing following objectives:

> 2) To explore the roles of the stakeholder in the education of Muslim girls.
>
> a. Exploring the role of Principal/ Head of the School as an EducationalStakeholder.

The schools are important educational stakeholder, who owes the responsibility of impartingquality education, The study investigate views of Principals/ Head of the schools in managing the schools, the infrastructural facilities in schools, the management of the teaching and the non-teaching staff, the developmental opportunities provided to the teachers through need-based training programmes with an intention in improvising the teacher's performance, which further contributes towards the quality education. The other notable stakeholder classified by the study are the higher secondary school teachers which paves the development of another sub objective:

> 2) To explore the roles of the stakeholder in the education of Muslim girls.
>
> b. Exploring the role of Higher Secondary School Teachers as anEducational stakeholder

This sub-objective identifies the views of higher secondary school teachers- as teachers arethe torch bearers of the nation, thus the study investigates the views of teachers on the availability of educational infrastructural facilities in school and its impact on teaching learning process, the trainings imparted to them, the encouragement and motivation provided to Muslim girls for higher education and their views on the higher educational prospects of the Muslim girls.

> 2) To explore the roles of the stakeholder in the education of Muslim girls.
>
> c. Exploring the role of Parents of Muslim girls as an Educational Stakeholder

Related to the education, the study recognizes Parents – as an educational stakeholder, who performs the role of influencer in the education. The influencing factor from the parental aspects are their educational qualification, their occupation, their views and attitudes towards the higher education of their daughters, their involvement, participation and support they extend towards the education of their daughters. The parental aspects weaved the thread for the development of following study subobjective:

Identifying another important stakeholder, the study categorized the community-who playsthe role of supporter in the educational progress through various sources like the beliefs andpractices followed by the community which has its impact on the mindset of the families, the support extended by community people such as encouraging the Muslim girls and supporting the educational process through monetary and non- monetary aids, which laid the development of following sub objective of the study.

---

2) To explore the roles of the stakeholder in the education of Muslim girls.

d. Exploring the role of Community as an Educational Stakeholder.

Any stakeholder cannot operate without the regulations of the governing bodies considering the educational stakeholder, the study categorizes the significant stakeholder- government by observing the applications and implementation of the government rules and regulations,the financial and non- financial assistance extended to the school authorities and to the Muslim girls as beneficiaries. This led to the thought of the following subobjective:

---

2) To explore the roles of the stakeholder in the education of Muslim girls.

e. Exploring the role of Government as regulator as an EducationalStakeholder

---

1.7 RESEARCH QUESTIONS:

1. Who are the stakeholders associated with the education of Muslim girls? 2.What are the roles stakeholders play in influencing education of Muslim girls?

2. What are the views of school Management related to the number of enrolments of Muslim girls in the higher secondary classes?

3. How has education influenced the attitude and aspirations of Muslim girls in the Vadodara district and around?

1.8 ETHICAL CONSIDERATION IN THE STUDY:

The primary ethical consideration of any research is to evade any harm or misleading the information shared by the respondents to the researcher. Incorporating the guidelines and principles of undertaking the research, the researcher has taken care while contacting the school authorities and conducting interviews with higher secondary Muslim girls as well as while interviewing their parents visiting their homes. The respondents participated in the study was consented for their participation and was also assured about their fortification of their identities.

Comprehensive discussion of the methodologies adopted for the study is discussed in the subsequent chapters of the study.

CHAPTER-II

Review of Literature

2.0 INTRODUCTION

A literature review done on any particular topic is the collection of the secondary literature done by various scholars over a period of time, which gives a researcher an outline of a particular topic. In this chapter, an effort is made to study the past literatures discussing the issues concerning the educational status of Muslims women, which ultimately has an impact over their socio-economic position in the community as a whole, and the later portion of the chapter explains the roles of various stakeholders, desired to improve the educational status of Muslim girls. In each sub themes the studies are arranged as per their year i.e., from the year 1980 to 2020.

Reviewed studies are classified as under:

a. Studies related to Muslim girl's education.
b. Studies related to Gender Equality and Empowerment.
c. Studies related to Islamic Perspectives on Education of Women.
d. Studies related to the Stakeholders in the Educational Institutions.

2.1 STUDIES RELATED TO MUSLIM GIRLS' EDUCATION

In this section twelve studies have been reviewed

Menon (1981) studied, "Status of Muslim women in India- A Case study of Kerala" studied educational status of Muslim women in four districts of Kerala- Calicut, Malappuram, Palghat, and Cannoneer, with the objective to find out the contribution of education in refining the social position of Muslim women in the district. Based on 1971 Census data, rural – urban stratification of the population was done; from each of the districts, using simple random sampling method 450 married women and 150 men – who were the decisionmakers of the family were interviewed using Interview schedule, designed separately both for men and women respondents. The simple frequency table and the chi square test and co- efficient of contingency was calculated for data analysis purpose. The outcomes of research highlighted the practice of solitude among the Muslim community as the chief reason for their educational backwardness. The study finds that from the Muslim households, girls arenot permitted to go outside their house, if there is no male member to escort them, thus the study further explains that because of the absence or no male members in the family as the reason, for school drop-out of many Muslim girls as one reason and many Muslim households were against sending their daughters in the co-education institutions as another important reason for the lower educational status in the selected districts of Kerala. The study also reveals that many Muslim household were still following the outmoded customsof early marriages and thus restricting Muslim girls from getting higher education. The studypoints the absence of male members in the family, lack of distinct educational institutions specifically for girls and the prevalence of early marriages as the chief reason for the lowereducational status of Muslim girls.

Siddiqui (1987), wrote on, "Muslim Woman in transition: a social profile", done with the main objective to look in the changes in terms of the educational attainment of Muslim women finds that the literacy level among Muslim females is less in comparison with the general women literacy rates from the rural areas. The study was done using survey method,stratifying the population in terms of their locality of residence i.e., urban and rural, and their socio-economic status.

Identifying the reason, the study points out the family condition as the responsible factors for the lower educational status, wherein the large number of respondents answered that they were not interested in education, while some others said that it is because of the lower socio-economic position of their family, they cannot receive education.

Mondal (1997) undertook a study on, "Educational status of Muslim: problems, prospects and priorities" in West Bengal, through field survey realities were gathered from six villages, and each village was different from other in terms of environmental setting. The study identified the educational status and the associated reasons of education among Muslims, the data of the study suggests that, only 68.22% of women were educated till primary, 27.63% were educated till secondary, whereas 3.55% of them were educated till higher secondary classes, and merely 0.75% of Muslim women were holding graduation degrees. The author says that the patriarchal structure of the society is the responsible factor, wherein the men folks of the community held the belief that, since women are never going to get in to the employment sector, it is futile wasting money in formal school education for women, they believe that the women should only be given the religious education and they should only have minimum knowledge of reading and writing.

Begum (1999), study on "Education and Muslim Women", undertaken with the objective to explore various factors responsible for educational backwardness among Muslim women in two villages of West Bengal also points out the same point that because of the acceptability and prevalence of the belief that women's and girls' should not be permitted to go outside their homes is the responsible factor for less education among women folk of the community. The study also reveals that the strict compliance of the purdah system, the lack of acceptance from the community towards the education of girls, lack of separate educational institutions for girls, more preference of girls in the household chores rather than the education, and the practice of early marriages withing the community becomes the obstacles in the way of Muslim girls.

Chaturvedi (2004) "Muslim Women and Development", the author scrutinizes participation of Muslim women in societal, financial, spiritual and other related developmental features. The study shows that the representation of Muslim females is genuinely very minimal at all school levels. The study emphasizes some of the important factor such as the prevalence of the belief that the girls should be taught domestic chores and should only be given Quranic education, deficiency of proper educational institutions for girls, purdah system, early marriages, and the prevalent socio- cultural views in the community thwarts the educational status of the females.

Hasan and Menon (2005) in five major Indian cities - Delhi, Aligarh, Calcutta, Hyderabadand Calicut, the study established the relation with the 'macro data', which was gathered by the authors by doing survey of Muslim women. The study was undertaken with the objectiveto detect and to bring association between the factors that determine the educational positionof Muslim women in these cities, by conducting field interviews. The findings of the studyreveal low educational status among Muslim women, specifying, that Muslim girls do take their enrolment in higher secondary classes but are unable to complete their education, andthese Muslim girls are forced to get married at an early stage than those of boys, Muslim parents gives more importance towards the education of their son rather than their daughters.

Pande (2006) on education of "Muslim women and girls in the slum areas of Hyderabad", was undertaken through survey method by using interview schedule and the case study method was adopted for collecting the data. The outcome of the research depict that the enrolment of Muslim girls was found to be optimum at the primary level, but the graph i.e., the number of girl's enrolment starts decreasing in secondary and higher secondary classes,the author through the case study method said that because of the fear of getting suitable marriage partner for their daughters, the parents do not prefer to send their daughters for higher secondary education and get them married at the early stage.

Parveen (2009) did a study "Exclusion of Muslim girls in School- A Participatory analysis in the district of Rampur", with the objective to examine the causes for controlling Muslim girls to Madrasa education only, the study's research style was exploratory in nature, the survey was undertaken in the four villages of Rampur district of Uttar Pradesh. The information was gathered through conducting Focus Group Discussions on a sample size of 1300 Muslim girls studying in schools. The information gathered was analyzed qualitatively, and the results suggest that because of presence of Muslim teachers in madrassa, considering madrassa as a safe environment for girls, and because of teacher's attitude in schools, girls of the Muslim community are only restricted towards madrassa education only.

Bhatt et, al (2011) on, "Islam: Gender and Education: A case study of Jammu and Kashmir", was undertaken by using secondary source of data from census 2001 and 2011 of the state of Jammu and Kashmir, in addition the supplementation of data is also done by State Digest of Statistics. The primary objective to explore the educational progress of Muslim women by comparing the situation of the earlier educational condition, with that of the current state, derived from secondary source of data. The study concluded that the educational state of women in the state of Jammu and Kashmir has shown considerable improvement as compared to the history, yet the registration of girls is found to be less, compared to the boys. The study point that though tremendous efforts are been made by the government, non- government, voluntary organization, yet large number of women in the state were illiterate.

Waseem (2012), "Muslim women Education and Empowerment in Rural Aligarh" was done in order to examine Muslim women in Aligarh's socio-economic and educational situation. The findings of the study depict the freedom and empowerment of women is mainly the outcome of the socio- cultural beliefs and practices rather than the religious faith and impositions and the study also clearly reveals a direct linkage of women's involvement in decision making, their socio- economic position is related with the type and the family structure.

Ahmed J (2016), undertook a study on "Problems and Prospects of Muslim women's Education: A sociological study of Poonch district of Jammu and Kashmir", the study adopted the exploratory and descriptive research design, with the sample size of 300 respondents, using multi stage sampling technique, from 15 villages of the district. The major focus of this research was to understand the educational position, problems, the nature of their problems, the attitudes of Muslim men towards the education of Muslim women. By using SPSS, simple frequency and cross tabulation the findings indicate, that educated parents, motivated their daughters for getting education, realizing the importance of education, the study noted noteworthy association between the educated husbands i.e the educated husbands expected their wives to be highly educated, thus this ultimately increase their age at marriage, the study also clearly brings distinction in thought process of educated and semi educated women of the district, as the educated women of the district favored co- educational institutions, whereas women's who had achieved some level of education were not willing for co-education and consider it as a harm for them.

Hussain (2018) The study on, "Educational status of Muslim women in India: Issues and challenges", with the intention to examine the educational position of Muslim women, to find out the issues and challenges faced by the Muslims in education, the study was based on secondary data and literature review and the findings suggested that the educational visualization of Muslims in India is still old-style, i.e Muslim community even today in the era of technological advancement do not consider education as an important change agent, they do not desire to give modern education to their daughters, rather prefer to send their daughters in Madrassa- who teach their students the syllabus which is out dated. Moreover, the study also reveals that there are few educated parents who give importance to daughter's education and aspire to give good education to their daughters, but the number of such parents is very minimal.

Saha S (2020) undertook a study on, "Educational Status of Muslim Women in West Bengal", with the aim of analyzing the educational advancement among Muslim women from the few blocks picked from the Nadia district, by surveying 150 households of the district, the teachers, the minority cell of the district , the survey was analyzed using simplefrequency table and graphical presentation, the findings indicates that in terms of education,Muslims are far behind , there is large number of drop-out rates among Muslim girls in higher secondary classes is more due to weak financial position, girls are still subjected to early marriages and orthodox beliefs and practices pertaining to the education of girls.

Overview of the studies related to education of Muslim women

Thus, from the above studies it can be inferred that the major factors for the lower educational status among Muslim community are the conservative beliefs and practices**, (Menon 1981; Siddiqui 1987; Begum 1999; Chaturvedi 2004**), less preference of daughter's education, (**Hasan and Menon 2005),** financial constraints, **(Chaturvedi 2004)**which are further accountable for the lower socio, economic, and cultural backwardness, **(Waseem 2012)** this backwardness can be eradicated from the society only through the medium of education which will bring empowerment among the females of the community.**(Saha 2020)**

2.2 STUDIES RELATED TO GENDER EQUALITY AND EMPOWERMENT

In this section review of ten studies is undertaken

Shah et, al (2011), carried out research on "A Study on Status of empowerment of Women in Jamnagar district", with the purpose to analyze the intensity of empowerment among women, the study adopted cross sectional research methodology. The data was gathered by using open ended questionnaire on a sample size of 150 respondents from different residential location of the city. The data was analyzed using statistical method and the results convey that participation of women in education and the employment leads to increase in their participation at domestic, economic and these women are free to take decisions related to their marriage and their family planning.

Chakraborty & Kundu (2012), "An Empirical analysis of women Empowerment within Muslim community in Murshidabad district of West Bengal" with the objective to represent the empirical analysis of empowerment of Muslim women. Survey method was adopted by the study, stratified random sampling was used as a sampling technique to gather the data from 150 women. Cumulative Empowerment Index and multiple linear regression technique as a method to analyze the situation and the results of this research indicate that Muslim women in the chosen district were selected for the study, are still unaware about their rights, their self- identity, and their self- esteem in the family pressure, this can be surmounted only through spreading awareness among the community and through education.

Talukdar (2015) studied, "Education and Empowerment of Muslim Women in West Bengal", with the objective to find out the educational status of Muslim women, their religious roles, and Muslim women inclusion in politics. The study was carried through descriptive study method, from the sample size of 400 Muslim women, with the help of questionnaires and interviews from the Muslim woman in Nadia district of West Bengal. The data so gathered was examined,

The study findings revealed that the process of bringing women empowerment among Muslim women is a very difficult task, as people are still facing economic scarcity in the families as a result unable to afford good education for their children, they are yet followers of the traditional beliefs and practices, which obstructs the educational progress of Muslim women.

Shazia (2016) studied, "Health and Empowerment: A Sociological Study of Women in Aligarh City", with the main purpose to find out the relationship between gender equality and empowerment, the study adopted quantitative as well as qualitative research methodology, with the help of structured and unstructured interview schedules and the casestudy method. In order to gather data from a sample size of 300 respondents, a purposive sampling approach was introduced. The analysis was done described through calculating percentage of the responses and the findings reveal that there is lack of empowerment among women, mostly women are involved in the workforce which is considered as casual work, no job security, partial and terrible work situation and absence of any social security arrangements, because of lack of education among women.

Barbhuyan (2017) studied, "Problems and Prospects of Muslim women in Higher Education", a descriptive study with 400 respondents with the main objective to find out the problems faced by Muslim women in higher education, their prospects for higher education, from those studying in higher education colleges. The data was gathered through self-structured questionnaire, and was analyzed using both structured and inferential statistics. The outcome of the research indicates that the most of the participants favored the higher education of Muslim women and said that the higher education of Muslim women will lead to social empowerment. economic self-dependence, economic empowerment, cultural empowerment, education as well as religious empowerment, however the educational status of Muslim women suffers because of various socio- cultural beliefs, practices like poverty, lack of education among parents, Psycho -fear of trailing their religious identity, the purdah system, the early marriages, the prevalence of dowry system, and other socio- cultural taboos and the conservative and orthodox mindset of people restricts the higher educational status of women.

Imtiyaz (2017), studied "Women Empowerment with special reference to Indian Women". The study objective was to find out the concurrent position of women empowerment, the empirical methodology was followed to conduct the study, & to choose the sample size of 200 respondents, a purposive sampling method was introduced. The researcher used an Empowerment scale as a research tool and the examination of the information was done by using t-test. The findings illustrate that reflecting empowerment in totality, the empowerment among working women is higher compared to non-working women, hence in order to bring about empowerment in the non-working women, who forms the larger segment of the society, only through education as a channel empowerment can be generated.

Saba et, al (2017), "Education as a powerful weapon for empowering Muslim women in West Bengal", The study assumed descriptive survey method to assess the empowerment of Muslim women belongs to the West Bengal. The data was collected from a sample of 500 Muslim women, using questionnaire as a research tool and Socio- Economic Status Scale. The assessment of the data was undertaken using statistical analysis. The study discloses that education and learning is the singular instrument, for giving strength to females to maketheir life at ease and giving them the power necessary for making determination about theirown life, about their own issues and pertaining to decisions of people related to them.

Biswas and Mukhopadyaya (2018), studied, "Marital Status and Women Empowerment in India", The study used the "National Family Health Survey (NFHS-3) data conducted during 2005-06", hence the secondary source of data was used, with the objective to analyzethe impact of marital status on women empowerment. Empowerment Index (EI) as well as Regression Analysis was used to draw examination of the results. The outcomes of this research indicates that the achieving the goal of gender equality and empowerment by the year 2015, laid down in Millennium Development Goals, represents the miserable position of Indian women, the social and cultural factors are more responsible for the status of women in Indian context, and the marital status of women in India is one of the determinantfactors of empowerment among Indian women across the communities.

A study on "Education and Empowerment of Muslim Women in the district of Murshidabad" by **Salam (2019)** undertaken to examine of the educational advancement and growth of Muslim women in the preferred district, and to find out the level of involvement of Muslim women in social, economic and political fronts. The study assumed social survey research method, by using questionnaire as research tool on the sample size of 400 Muslim women selected through purposive sampling technique. The data was analyzed through frequency and percentages and the findings of the study indicated that 60% of Muslim women were not involved in any occupation but they were housewives, less than 20% of women in Murshidabad are in the political and economic spheres, women show no interest and involvement in the economic and political activities.

Habib et, al (2019) studied, "Impact of Education and Employment on Women Empowerment". The key purpose of this research was to study the effects of women's liberation in Quetta, the study followed survey method and the information was gathered from the respondents through questionnaire as a research tool, non-probability convenient sampling method was applied to fetch the data from the sample size of 316 educated, employed and self-employed women living in Quetta. The findings of the study were analyzed using descriptive method and SPSS, the result describes that engagement of women in workforce increase their involvement in decision making process at the domestic as well as at communal stages, as it results in intensifications of women's earning capacity which help them to have improved health and will also be able to educate their children and other family members.

Overview of the studies related to Gender equality and Empowerment

In light of the above referred studies, it can be construed that the position of Muslim women in India is discouraging, **(Chakraborty & Kundu 2012; Barbhuyan 2017)** a lot of effort is needed to the change the mindset of the community, **(Chakraborty & Kundu 2012)** which even today in the era of modernization, industrialization, the community is not focusing on the empowerment of women-who forms the larger segment of the communityand hence the community as a whole performs the 'Invisible' and 'Marginal' role towards the nation's development. The studies also indicate that Muslim women do have awareness about their rights and duties, but they are controlled by their male members hence the process of bringing empowerment among women is a mission in itself. **(Imtiyaz 2017; Salam 2019)**

2.3 STUDIES RELATED TO ISLAMIC PERSPECTIVES ON EDUCATION OF WOMEN

In this section review of five studies is considered

Brookfield M (2013) undertook a study on "The Impacts of Education: A Case Study of Muslim Women in Ngaoundéré, Cameroon", with the objective to study the impact of modern education on Muslim women in Ngaoundéré. The study adopted the qualitative research methodology, through conducting survey of 150 Muslim women residing in Ngaoundéré, the data was analyzed qualitatively by drawing inferences from the respondent's interview.

The study findings indicates that the educational status among Muslim women is increasingin Cameroon, women are increasing their age of marriages and are attaining education, theyare entering in to the workforce and are living socially, economically independent life, because of the realization among majority of Muslim community that there is no such religious obligation which constrain a female in to the four walls of the residence and prescribe the responsibility of upbringing of children only to the females.

Galloway S (2014) conducted a study on "The Impact of Islam as a Religion and Muslim women on Gender Equality: A Phenomenological Research Study" aimed at investigating and exploring the connotations, structures, and the spirit of the survived involvements of Muslim women while looking to gain knowledge of how Islam, as a religion, endorse gender parity through an Islamic scriptural (Kalam) background. The key intention behind this phenomenological research is to generate a comprehensive explanation of the subsisted knowledges of "Muslim women while proceeding and understanding of how Islam, as a religion, can encourage gender equality for Muslim women". The study espoused qualitative research design framework, by gathering data through semi-structured interview, through researcher's observations and recorded interviews of 100 Muslim women by adopting the purposive sampling technique, of selecting only women above 18 years of age. The analysis of the data gathered was done through open ended coding system by relating the responses as shared by the respondents. The findings of the study focusing on the gender equality in terms of gaining education revealed that improved and considerate understanding of Islam, as a religion, can serve as a process of updating other people of the community, the governmental and non- governmental agencies, which will useful in improving the lives of Muslim women and will bring the educational progress, increase their participation in the workforce as well as will also increase their participation in politics as well.

Fauzia (2017) in a study titled, "Right to education: status of Muslim girl children in rural Uttar Pradesh", that according to Islam there is no discrimination between genders in terms of acquiring education, she refers the history by stating that the women in Islam have really recognized themselves through education in the past, adding to it she also narrates that Islam not only restrict on getting religious education, in- fact it does provide equality of getting knowledge and learning for both the genders. The key aim of the study was to investigate multiple reasons responsible for dropping out of school for Muslim girls and to interview Muslim girls' parents and teachers and vulnerable groups. For the purpose of data collection, this study followed survey methods from the sample size of 419 girl students and 354 girls' parents.

Noorain (2018) studied, "Islam on Women Education", with the objective to study the Quranic verses on women's education, the data were gathered from a sample of 500 respondents via a questionnaire by using purposive sampling technique from the city of Lucknow. The analysis of the data was carried through factor analysis and the findings mentions the educational inferences that Islam as religion has stressed the concept of genderequality, and has made tremendous efforts in spreading awareness among women folks pertaining to their rights, and also has given freedom to develop the individual's personality,hence there is no restrictions on both the gender on attaining education and for developmentof self.

Overview of the studies emphasizing the Islamic perspective on education

Review of studies focusing the Islamic perspectives on education , it can be inferred that thethere are no restrictions imposed on Muslim women on gaining education,**(Fauzia 2017)** in fact the religion is very affirmative and emphasizes on participation of Muslim women inboth the education as well as in the employment sector, **(Noorain 2018)** but because of theprevalence and acceptance of the cultural and social beliefs and practices, **(Barbhuyan 2017)** is the reason for the marginalized segment of the population, hence, education is theonly weapon to bring change in the community, thus it is necessary to spread correct knowledge among the masses about the religious beliefs and practices, **(Chakraborty & Kundu 2012)** hence the association and active support of all stakeholders is needed to bringtransformation towards the educational status of the Muslim community and specifically for the females and girls.

2.4 STUDIES RELATED TO THE STAKEHOLDERS IN THE EDUCATIONAL INSTITUTIONS

It is said that the education as a process demands mutual interaction between all the associated stakeholders such as the school administrators and executives, the parents, the government and significant others who are directly or indirectly associated with the educational institutions.

For the purpose of the current study, review of the studies is classified as under

a. School – as an Educational Stakeholder
b. Parents- as an Educational Stakeholder
c. Community- as an Educational Stakeholder
d. Government- as an Educational Stakeholder

2.4.1 SCHOOL AS AN EDUCATIONAL STAKEHOLDER

For the purpose of the study, the studies in this section are categorized as under

a. Studies related to infrastructural development in schools
b. Studies related to the teaching quality, the professional development opportunities, incentives of teachers
c. Studies related to the academic, social and psychological development of students

2.4.1 a) STUDIES RELATED TO INFRASTRUCTURAL DEVELOPMENT IN SCHOOLS

In this section review of seven studies is undertaken

Mangipudy & Venkata, (2010), "The Impact of eliminating extraneous sound and Light on Student's Achievement", by the authors test their hypothesis on the effect on student performance by removing sound and light. The analysis was performed on the sample size of 148 secondary section students, by adopting Campbell and Stanley's (1963) non- equivalent control group and the data was analyzed through using ANOVA test. The outcomes of the research states that the school having good infrastructural facilities will produce good outcome in comparison with the school which is poorly equipped with infrastructural facilities.

Mylliemngap (2011) studied "A Study of Infrastructural Facilities of Secondary Schools inShillong Town", with the objective to study the problems faced due to infrastructural facilities, its effects on the performance of teachers and student's academic performance, from 10 secondary schools in Shillong, using simple random sampling methods to provide the sample size of 100 respondents. The data was collected through questionnaires and was analyzed in terms of percentage. The study findings reveal that the school are an important educational institution, it is necessary for the schools to have adequate basic as well as educational infrastructural facilities in schools such as the libraries, computer labs, science, physics, math's lab according to the subjects offered by the schools, as the infrastructural facilities in school have a significant relationship with the students' academic success as well as it also has its effect on the deliverance of teachers.

Nepal B (2016) studied, "Relationship Among School's Infrastructure Facilities, Learning Environment and Student's Outcome", with the objective to analyze, the association between the infrastructural facilities in school, learning atmosphere and the outcome of students. The data was gathered from a sample size of 320 respondents, from 40 secondary schools, by using questionnaire as tool for gathering the data. The data so gathered was analyzed using multi regression table. The results suggest that there is a clear association between the provision of school resources and the outcome of the student's academic achievement.

Boruah (2017) studied, "A Study on availability of Educational Facilities for the Teachersand the students", with the main objective to find the physical facilities available in government schools for teachers and students, the study adopted descriptive research methodology. Tabular form of data analysis was adopted for the study, to ascertain the studyresults gathered from the sample size of 20 government primary schools using questionnaires as a research instrument. The study reveals that the majority of the primary schools selected for the study are deficient of basic infrastructural facilities such as peripheryof the school premises, head instructors' room, students' common room, proper playgroundetc. and these are the causative factor in the high students drop out rate in primary schooling,thus the government schools lack basic facilities in the school premises.

Ummer and Shanmugam (2017) studied, "A Study on Infrastructural Facilities in Schools of Kulgam District (J&K)". The aim of the research was "to examine the status of educational infrastructure facilities in the district of Kulgam. The study was conducted usingmulti-stage random sampling technique on the sample size of 100, and the data were examined using compound growth rate, annual growth rate and percentage". The findings indicates that nearly 70% of the schools chosen for the study lacks educational facilities in school and considered it as important determinant for lower literacy level, moreover the school authorities only were not contended with the facilities, which affects their performance as well.

Chaudhari N and Nagwanshee R (2019) did "A comparative study between Rural and Urban Schools with special reference to Infrastructural facilities", the study was undertakenwith the intention, to make comparison of the availability of educational infrastructural facilities in rural and urban schools. The study followed survey method in the Annupur district of Madhya Pradesh by using questionnaire as a research tool. The descriptive way of data analysis using measures of central tendency was used for the analysis. The study's results indicate that there is a substantial association between the availability of the infrastructural facilities in school and teacher's retention.

2.4.1 b) STUDIES RELATED TO THE TEACHING QUALITY, PROFESSIONALDEVELOPMENT OPPORTUNITIES, INCENTIVES OF TEACHERS

In the current criteria, five studies have been reviewed

Alvarez (2008) studied "The Relationship of Teacher Quality and Student Achievement inElementary Schools from the New York City", the analysis can be defined as a cross- sectional research sample using the survey approach, with the objective to examine how the characteristics of teachers affect the student's performance. For the analysis of data, multi- variate analysis and multiple regression analysis experiments were performed. The findingsof the study suggest that there is strong association between the characteristics of teachers on students' academic results, moreover the research also points out the important fact that the educational qualification of teachers, their engagement in professional development activities also affects the student's performance.

Lee (2013) studied, "Professional development and Teacher's perception of Efficacy and Inclusion", with the intention to identify association among the teacher's professional development and self-efficacy. The sample size of the study was 385 teachers from the elementary school by using purposive sampling, the data was gathered by using two different scales- Teacher's Activity Survey and Teacher's Efficacy for Inclusion survey. The data was analyzed used quantitative survey methods and the findings indicate that professional development opportunities for the teachers are very significant in bringing theeffective classroom teaching.

Sekhar, Reddy and Nagarjuna (2014) studied, "A Study of Teacher's Motivation of Teachers in Relation to Certain

Factors", with an intention to find out the impact of management, locality, and qualification on the teacher's motivation. The data required for the study was collected from 160 teachers using questionnaire as a research tool and using stratified random sampling method for selecting the sample size. Inferential statistical techniques were used to assess the data. The Study findings points out that the performance and motivation of teachers is affected by aspects such as the kind of management, the type of locality of schools and their educational qualification.

Lawrence and Hanitha (2017), conducted research entitled "A Study on Teachers' Motivational Strategy and Academic Achievement of Higher Secondary Students". The analysis was carried out using the survey approach in order to investigate the association between teacher motivational technique and academic performance of higher secondary students. On a sample size in Kancheepuram educational district of 600 higher secondary school students studying. The research followed a basic random sampling technique for collecting the findings by using the self-made Teachers' Motivational Approach Scale and using the marks won by the students in the quarterly exams as academic achievement. For the estimation and explanation of outcomes, percentage analysis, standard deviation, mean,t-test and correlation analysis were used. The findings of the study notes that students studying in government schools are academically good compared to those studying in unaided and aided schools and there between was a strong association between motivational approach of the teacher and academic success of students.

Baluyos (2019) studied, "Teachers' Job Satisfaction and Work Performance".

A descriptive correlational study was undertaken with the objective to verify the affiliation on the teachers' level of job satisfaction and their work performance. Statistical analysis was used for the purpose of assessing the data, which was collected from the sample 313 school teachers using questionnaire as research instrument. The research findings indicate that the work performance of the teachers is inversely affected by the head of the school, and their guidance and precisely affected by the teachers' job security.

2.4.1 c) STUDIES RELATED TO THE ACADEMIC, SOCIAL AND PSYCHOLOGICAL DEVELOPMENT OF STUDENTS

To bring about the effectiveness of school, it is necessary to have appropriate and relevant curriculum, providing the students to develop their academic, social as well psychological skills, in this section six studies have been reviewed:

Zigarelli (1996) studied, "An empirical test of conclusions from effective schools", the test included effective school variable from the past literature and was tested empirically on student's achievement. The data was collected from the "National Educational Longitudinal" study, and the regression analysis was done on the sample size of 160 schools which indicates that the availability of qualified teachers, adequate participation and satisfaction of teachers, the contributions and the leadership ability of the school principal, maintenance of culture of consistent academic prosperity of school, Co-operative and healthier relationship among the school administration, and parents' interest in the education of their children are the important factor determining the academic development of students.

Preetham (2008), studied "Co-Curricular activities, attitudes and participation of Secondary school students", with the major objective to study student's participation and attitudes towards co- curricular activities, data from 40 high schools in the Guntur district of Andhra Pradesh was collected, wherein, 20 students from each school were randomly selected, and the information generated was examined by using frequencies, descriptive, t- tests, ANOVA and correlations. The findings of the study suggest that through participationin co- curricular activities students gain insight of the practical problem-solving skill which brings overall development of a child.

Annu S and Mishra S (2013) studied "Impact of Extra-Curricular activities on students in private schools of Lucknow district", with the primary objective of the research is to examine involvement of students in various extra- curricular activities and optimistic outcome in their performance. For the data collection, a purposeful sampling approach wasused, using questionnaire as a tool from the study of 60 school-going students. Using statistical analysis, the data was analyzed and the result states that participation of childrenin extra-curricular activities have positive effect on student's lives as it improves their overall behavior, school performance and also enhance their social skills.

Rabiya (2017) studied, "Psychological Wellbeing, Study Involvement and Academic Environment of Government and Private Secondary School Students – A Comparative Study". The primary objective of the research is to examine the affiliation between psychological wellbeing, study immersion, academic environment, and academic achievement of the students from secondary school. The analysis was carried out on the sample size of 240 high school students selected through random sampling technique, Psychological Wellbeing scale, learning style inventory, School environment inventory, was used to collect the information, analyzed using t-test, percentage, mean and standard deviation. The study findings convey that the school atmosphere has a substantial correlation with Psychological Health and Learning Styles of students; better the environment, better will be the learning process, hence it is essential for schools to furnish unobstructed environment to assist students to work free.

Singh, A. (2017) undertook a study on "Effect of Co-Curricular Activities on Academic Achievement of Students". The purpose of the research was to define the effect of extracurricular activities on the academic performance of students. Non- probability sampling method was adopted from the sample size of 100 respondents and the data was collected through checklist, the result reveals that the participation of students in extra-curricular activities have a significant relation with their academic achievements.

Abdullah (2017) on "The Relationship between Social Skills, Self-Esteem and Big Five Personality Factors among Children", the aim of this study is to examine the relationship between social skills and personality variables, the data was collected from 225 school goingchildren, by adopting "Social Skills Measure and Rosenberg Self Esteem Scale", and the results were analyzed using descriptive parameters and statistical correlation, standard deviation. The study findings illustrate that there exists a noteworthy relationship between the social skills such as "taking criticism, showing respect, problem solving, following rights and responsibilities, and assertiveness, with the following Big Factors of Personality: Extraversion, Agreeableness, Conscientiousness, and Openness".

Overview of the studies related to Schools an Educational Stakeholders

From the above referred studies, it can be inferred that a school is an important educational stakeholder performs the role of facilitator in rendering quality education through its proper administration **(Zigarelli 1996; Rabiya 2017)**, through providing the required and appropriate infrastructural facilities **(Mangipudy 2010; Mylliemngap 2011; Nepal 2016)**, which not only benefits and attracts students towards the school premises, but it also helps in retention and improves performance of the teachers **(Chaudhari and Nagwanshee 2019; Sekhar et.al 2014; Baluyos 2019)**. Moreover, schools by also providing developmental opportunities for the teachers, **(Lee 2013)** giving them proper incentives will motivate teachers to work and thus, they will be able to impart quality education, by adopting proper curriculum and also by encouraging students in participation in extra-curricular activities **(Preetham 2008; Annu and Mishra 2013; Singh 2017)**, which bring about wholistic development of students. This further will increase the level of educational status and will also bring the school effectiveness, for instance, **Chhaya M (1998)** says in her paper, "Effective Schools", A paper from "Contemporary Thoughts on Education", successful schools cultivate passion for learning, critical thinking, skills for problem solving, aesthetic appreciation, curiosity and imagination, and leadership skills. For their children, parents want a full education. What is expected is that our young people become educated and educated residents who are willing to actively engage in our social and economic life and are not merely qualified employees with minimal capacity for such involvement.

2.4.2 PARENTS AS AN EDUCATIONAL STAKEHOLDERS

The next important stakeholder in the education sector after the educational institutions is the parents of the child, it is said that the best teacher of a child is the child's parents. Before a child widens his/ her horizon towards the school, the child acquires through observation and interaction lot of new knowledge from the parents. This idea is also very much supported by various studies undertaken to address the influence of parents in child's development, this section of the review categorizes the study as mentioned:

a. Studies related to Socio-economic status of parents
b. Studies related to educational status of parents
c. Studies related to occupation of parents
d. Studies related to attitudes of parents and their involvement in children's education.

2.4.2 a) STUDIES RELATED TO SOCIO-ECONOMIC STATUS OF PARENTS

In this section review of seven studies are undertaken

Sirin, (2005), "Socioeconomic Status and Academic Achievement: A Meta Analytic Review of Research", the literature published during the period (1990-2000) on socio- economic status and students' academic achievements was extensively reviewed. From 74 independent samples, the sample consisted of "101,157 students, 6,871 schools, and 128 school districts. The result concluded that the socio-economic status and the educational progress of students correlate between medium and strong".

Muhammed A and Akanle (2008) carried research on, "Socio-economic factors influencing students' academic performance in Nigeria", the aim is to identify the impact of socio-economic status of the parents' on students' educational progress, the study was undertaken by a survey method, using questionnaire as a tool by choosing a sample of 120 respondents. The results were statistically analyzed and confirmed the findings that the income of parents and the academic achievement of students of secondary and junior secondary school students. The study supports the findings that the lower parental income will not be able to meet with the needs of their children's education, and which has significant impact in their classroom performance, results in lower concentration level, lower perception, lower academic performance, frustration, emotional disturbance among students, which results in their withdrawal from schools, especially because the children's educational need is not addressed by parents.

Memon G.R, et, al (2010), A study on, "Impact of Parental Socio-economic status on student's educational achievements at secondary schools of District Malir, Karachi" with the primary objective of figuring out the relationship between the socio-economic condition of the parents and its effect on the academic performance of students enrolled in matriculation. The study undertaken was a descriptive study based on the empirical data, and using questionnaire as a research tool. Purposive sampling technique was used, and thus the study was undertaken with the sample size of 240 students. The data was statistically analyzed and revealed that the socio- economic position of the parents is the most unescapable factor towards the educational progress of the children, as it comprises ofall the essential facilities including like electricity facility and other supporting facility in the child's residence.

Huisman, Rani, and Smits, (2010) in a working paper on "keeping children in school: Household and district-level determinants of school dropout in 363 districts of 30 developing countries". In their research, they considered the role of socio-economic, cultural, and educational infrastructure characteristics in primary school enrolment, with a sample size of 70,000 children residing in 439 districts of 26 states of India. It is derived from the findings of the study that in majority of the cases (around 70%) the enrolment decision of students in the school is relied on the socio-economic position of the parents within the child's household. The study also brought in to comparison of the residence of children living in urban areas (cities) to that of those living in rural areas, and highlights thefact that in rural areas, the decision of sending a child to school is the most decisive decisionbased on the socio-economic status of the parents, particularly the decision is majorly affected in cases where the number of school and the teachers in schools is less, and also ifthere is patriarchal dominance within the rural area, the children specially girl child will becomparatively less in number in rural schools

Chandra R and Azimuddin S (2013), studied "Influence of Socio-Economic Status on Academic Achievement of Secondary School Students of Lucknow City, to analyze the socio-economic status and academic performance of parents, the data was collected from 14secondary school students", comprising the sample size of 614 students. The Socio- Economic Status Scale (2004) was used for the purpose of data collection, the collected datawas analyzed using Karl Pearson correlation coefficient and t- test, and the results convey that the socio-economic status of parents is closely linked to students' academic success.

Singh P and Chaudhary G (2015), "Impact of Socio-economic status on academic achievement of school students", the goal is to recognize the effect of the socio-economic status of parents on the academic success of students. Using the normative survey method, the study was carried out using the Socio-Economic Status Scale on a sample of 450 respondents studying higher secondary classes. The findings of the research were analyzed using mean, standard deviation and ANOVA test, the outcome highlighted the important association between the socio-economic status of parents and their academic achievement,

i.e., higher socio-economic status, higher academic performance.

Musangu M (2017) in the research entitled, "Parental Socio-economic Status and Academic Performance of Secondary School Students in the Western Province of Republic of Zambia", they analyzed the association between parental income and academic success of high school students. 500 respondents were chosen for the analysis using a basic random sampling method, questionnaires were used to gather the data and the data were analyzed using SPSS, and the findings found that the academic success of students is impacted by the socio-economic status of parents.

2.4.1 b) STUDIES RELATED TO EDUCATIONAL STATUS OF PARENTS

In this section review of five studies is undertaken

Bhatnagar and Sharma (1992) on, "A Study of the Relationship Between Parental Education and Academic achievement in a Semi- Rural Setting" was undertaken to find outthe connection between students' parental education and academic achievement. The research was conducted in the semi-rural setting of Rajasthan with a sample size of 185 students from 9, 10, and 11 standards. Statistical analysis was used to draw findings of the study, which indicate that education of parents is a very important factor towards the academic achievement of children.

Kaur (2011) studied, "A study of academic achievement of school students having illiterateand literate parents", the study was collected through a descriptive survey method on the sample size of 100 school students from government schools in Hoshiarpur district of Punjab with the aim of studying the academic progress of the students in relation to their parents' educational status. The data was collected through Personal data form and was analyzed by frequency distribution, the results said that students of literate parents were good in their academic's performance, unlike those students whose parents were illiterate.

Vellymallay (2011) studied, "A Study of the relationship between Indian parents' educational level and their involvement in their children's education". The study was conducted primarily to explore the association between the educational status of Indian parents with their interest in their children's education. The study analysis was carried out on a sample size of 150 Indian students who were picked by stratified random sampling technique in Indian schools. The data was collected by using structured interview schedulesand questionnaires which was assessed by using SPSS and the findings of the study noted advanced educational status of parents, the higher expectation from their children in terms of the educational achievement, parents with higher educational status inclined to implement the novel tactics in keeping their children engrossed at home and adopts ways which paves excellence in their performance at school as well. Hence the study remarks that the educational status of parents plays and important role towards the academic achievement of children.

Ogunshola & Adewale (2012) observed the influence of parental socio-economic status on student academic achievement in a study entitled, "The Effects of Parental Socio-Economic Status on Academic Performance of Students in Selected Schools in Edulga of Kwara State Nigeria". Samples from three schools in Kwara state was randomly selected, and the by applying the ANOVA and t-test, the results were configured. The findings suggest that there is no association between the academic success of students and the socio-economic status of parents, but it is more affected by the educational qualification of the parent and the healthy state of mind and body of children.

Qadri (2018) studied, "Parental Educational Status and Academic Achievement of Students", to investigate the association between parents' educational status and children's academic achievements at secondary level. The study adopted a survey method and used Performa as a research device to collect the data from the sample size of 500 secondary school students randomly. The data was analyzed using chi square test and percentage analysis and confirmed that the educational status of both the parents plays a very pivotal role towards the educational achievement of students as their educational influence is high on the students.

2.4.2 c) STUDIES RELATED TO OCCUPATIONAL STATUS OF PARENTS

In this section review of five studies is undertaken.

Saifullah and Mehmood, (2011) studied, "Effects of Socioeconomic Status on Students Achievement", the study examines the influence of income and occupation on educational accomplishment of students, in three different colleges of Gujarat, the data was gathered using questionnaire as a tool and was analyzed through frequency percentage. The results conclude that about 60.02% of children performed well in academic, whose parents are employed in government jobs than those employed in private jobs, as the government jobs are more secure than the jobs in private sector. Another finding of the study, towards the education of mother points that about 64.5 % of students whose mothers were employed in to the government sector performed better, hence the study brings out the occupational statusof both father and the mother have their immense contribution towards the education of their children.

Rajitha (2011) undertook a study on, "Study on the Influence of Parental Education and Occupation on the Achievement Motivation of adolescents", with the goal of figuring out the impact of parental education on the desire of adolescents to accomplish, the study usedpretested the reliability and validity scales on the sample size of 588 respondents. Varianceand statistical analysis were used to derive the results, which states that the education of parents greatly influence the academic achievement, and also motivates the students.

Faisal, (2014) studied "Influence of Parent Socio-Economic Status on their Involvement atHome", the study was undertaken to explore "socio economic status of parents" and their involvement at home, the data was collected from the sample size 150 students using purposive convenient method, by using questionnaire as a research tool which was analyzed using SPSS. The study supports the findings that parent's involvement in to 'prestigious occupation' increase the tendency of their contribution towards their children academic performance by helping their children in day-to-day activities of school and at home. Mitigating the reason, he says that the occupation that parents are involved in to is a determinant aspect about their financial position.

Walter (2018) A study on "Influence of Parental Occupation and Parental income on students' Academic performance in Public Day Secondary Schools" with the intention to find out the impact of parental occupation on the academic performance of students, the data was gathered from 210 respondents using stratified and simple random sampling technique, using questionnaire as a study tool. Using descriptive and inferential statistics, the data was analyzed. The findings constrained the fact that parental employment had a major impact on students' academic performance rather than on parents' educational background.

Moneva, Rozado and Sollano (2019) studied, "Parents Occupation and Students' Self- esteem", with the purpose to identify the association between the professional background of parents and the self-esteem of students. The study followed descriptive design to collect the data from the sample size of 245 respondents through using questionnaire as a research instrument examined through ANNOVA test. The study findings indicate that the self-esteem of students is not related with the occupational status of parents, but students with high self-esteem and good occupational status of parents will be able to use their self-esteemto chase their aspirations.

2.4.2 d) STUDIES RELATED TO THE INVOLVEMENT OF PARENTS AND THEFAMILY STRUCTURE

In this section review of four studies is undertaken

Muthoni (2013) studied, "Relationship Between Family Background and Academic Performance of Secondary Schools Students: A Case of Siakago Division, Mbeere North District, Kenya", with an objective to study the connection between the size of the family and its influence on students' academic achievement.

To select the sample size of 338 participants, the study followed a stratified random sampling method and the data was collected using a questionnaire as a research tool. The students were analyzed with descriptive and inferential statistics and the results of the study show that children belonging to large families are weaker in their academic performance than those belonging to large families.

Giri (2014) studied, "A Comparative Study on The Academic Achievement of Secondary Level Students of Joint and Nuclear Families in Relation to their values and adjustment". The primary objective of the research is to compare the academic performance of students belonging to joint family than those coming from the nuclear families. The study gathered its data from three districts comprising of a sample size of 585 students studying in class XII of Uttar Pradesh. The study used pretested tools for the data collection and the data wasexamined by applying t- test and ANOVA test, and the results of the study indicates that the students belonging to nuclear families are better in the academic performances compared to students from the joint families.

Vijayalakshmi and Muniappan (2016) carried a study on, "Parental Involvement and achievement of school students", to find out the relationship between parental involvement and the achievement of students in secondary school. A cross sectional descriptive correlational research design was adopted on a sample size of 200 respondents using purposive sampling technique method. The data was collected through pretested tools and was statistical analysis was used. The findings represent the significant association between the parental interest in children's schooling and their class results.

Prema (2016), studied "Parental Involvement in Relation with Academic Achievement of Progeny", to investigate the involvement of children in education of children belonging to the age group of 11- 17 years and their academic accomplishment. The study adopted descriptive survey method and used questionnaire to collect the data from a sample size of 92 parents selected through simple random sampling technique.

Overview of the studies related to Parents as an Educational stakeholders

It can be summarized that the all the associated factors such as socio-economic condition (**Sirin 2005; Memon 2009; Chandra and Azimuddin 2013; Singh and Chaudhary 2015;Musangu 2017**), the financial position (**Muhammed & Akanle 2008**), the education of parents (**Bhatnagar & Sharma 1992; Kaur 2011; Vellymallay 2011; Rajitha 2011; Ogunshula & Adewale 2013; Qadri 2018**), the occupation (**Saifullah & Mehmood 2011; Faisal 2014;**

Walter 2018; Monevo et.al 2019) , the parental involvement **(Vijayalakshmi&Muniappan 2016; Prema 2016)** and the family structures **(Muthoni 2013; Giri 2014)**, have its impact on the education of children. On reviewing studies, thus, it can be said that the parents are the important pillars and perform the role as an influencer in the education of children. Referring to the study conducted by **Parveen (2009-10)** titled, "Exclusion of Muslim Girls from Schools- A Participatory analysis in the district of Rampur", it can be said that parents are the important support pillar in the education of their Muslim daughters,the girls are deprived of education because of the parental attitudes towards the education of their daughter. Not only the socio-economic background, the education, the parental occupation but their attitudes and involvements matter a lot with regard to achievement of children in general and specifically for girl child.

2.4.3 COMMUNITY AS AN EDUCATIONAL STAKEHOLDER

In this section review of four studies is undertaken

Baradei L and Amin K (2010) in their study titled, "Community Participation in Education: A case study of the board of trustees experience in Fayoum governerate in Egypt". An empirical study was conducted based on structured interviews by adopting purposive sampling technique on a sample size of 52 board members. The study supports that role of school is definitely very important for bringing quality education, but it is also to be recognized that the school solely will not be able to perform this function effectively,it does require the assistance of various community people to enrich students learning.

Nirmala K and Selvi P (2012), as a pilot effort to include/improve community engagement in schools to validate the best organizational environment in primary schools, an experimental study was performed in the Madurai District, in a study titled "Promoting Smart Schools with Community Participation- An Experimental Study at the Grassroots in India", the study scrutinizes the working of the VECs (Village Educational Committees) in selected villages. The data was selected from 50 households selected through random sampling technique method. The findings of the study states that through involvement of VEC in school decision making, there was a positive change in the attitudes of people and they started owning and taking right decision for schools, which ultimately reduced the absenteeism from school of both the teachers as well as the students.

Narwana (2015) studied "A global approach to school education and local reality: A case study of community participation in Haryana", with the objective to find the impact of "community participation in the school education" through qualitative research methodology and by doing field survey and case study method. The study concludes by stating that the institutions which are established to engage in the school participation are not able to justify their involvement, hence the involvement of such institutions in the schoolmanagement makes no impact on the educational outcome of the students.

Kusumaningrum et, al (2017) studied, "Community participation in improving Educational Quality", with the objective to find out the role of community in terms of improving educational quality, the study adopted descriptive study design by using questionnaire as a research tool and selecting a sample size of 54 public and private elementary school by using proportional group sampling technique. SPSS and correlation were used to evaluate the data collected. The findings reveal that active community involvement helps in the development of schools and towards imparting quality education.

Overview of studies related to community as an Educational Stakeholder.

The literature review in this context, specifies that the community can play an important role as the supporter for rendering quality education. Relevant community participation **(Baradei &Amin 2010)** can help the educational institutions by giving practical exposuresto the related subjects and can develop a sense of ownership among community members, which will create enthusiasm and motivation among students, the parents, the staff. The community can be supportive in spreading awareness about the importance of education andcan be an effective medium of spreading education, however, such studies are very limited,the studies so far reviewed focus on merely the involvement of community in school management, and to some extent the involvement is not able to meet the objective as pointed by **Narwana (2015).**

2.4.4 GOVERNMENT AS AN EDUCATIONAL STAKEHOLDER

In this section one review of study is undertaken

A study on "Stakeholders Perception of the Sarva Shiksha Abhiyan Effectiveness in increasing school enrolment in India **Vayaliparampil (2012).** The objective of the study investigates in what way varied stakeholders engaged with school enrolments recognize the efficacy of the Sarva Shiksha Abhiyan in increasing school enrolment in India.

The Study explores various intercessions programmes like mid- deal programme, stipend for girls, school sanitation and hygiene education, madrassa modernization, civil works, village education committee, residential hostel for girls and school supplies. The study embraced multiple case study design to conduct the research by using photovoice and semi-structured interviews on a sample size of 183 respondents, comprising of state and district officials, education officers, international NGO officers, local NGO officers, teachers, and parents. A phenomenological approach and thematic analysis were employed to analyze the data. The findings of the study suggest that Mid-day Meal programme is more effective intervention. It was also stated that obstacles in executing the Sarva Shiksha Abhiyan were the misuse of funds, mishandling of school facilities and the inadequacy of personnel, moreover the programme was unproductive in addressing secondary school enrolment challenges of loss of income, deprived quality of schooling and the safety of girls.

Overview of the study related to government as an educational stakeholder.

From the above referred study, it can be inferred that the government in Indian context, both central as well as the state plays a very significant role through implementing programmes and schemes, however the effective implementation is a result of lack of accomplishment of levied schemes and programmes. There are various other varied schemes and programmes laid down by the central government to raise the educational status of girls and specifically of Muslim girls, there is a need to focus on the accomplishments of the objectives of the levied programmes as well, however, such studies are very few.

Table:2.0 Gap Analysis of Literature review Studies

Area	Studies from ROL	Study Findings
Studies related to the education of Muslim Woman	Mondal 1997	The study points the data on the educational level of males and females in the area of the study and highlights the belief that the women should only be given the religious education andthey should only have minimum knowledge of reading and writing. **Gap**: The study is not providing the data on how many women are accepting this patriarchal belief and supporting this belief within the community.
Studies related to the education of Muslim Woman	Begum 1999 Chaturvedi 2004;	The studies highlight social and cultural factors responsible for the lower educational status among Muslim community. **Gap**: The studies lack to take in to consideration economic factors.

Studies related to the education of Muslim Woman	Hasan and Menon 2005 Pande 2006	The study was undertaken to explore the educational position of Muslim women in metrocities. **Gap**: The comprehensive aspect like the socio-economic position, their occupational level is not taken in to consideration, which is one of the detrimental factors
Studies related to the education of Muslim Woman	Parveen 2009	The study finds that because of presence of Muslim female teachers in madrassa, they are only restricted towards madrassa education only **Gap**: The study lacks exploration of the availability and accessibility of educational institutions in the area covered under the study
Studies related to Gender Equality and Empowerment	Imtiyaz (2017)	The study brings out the comparative viewof level of empowerment among working and Non-working Muslim women. **Gap**: The study lack clarity inreflecting the correct picture i.e to say that which is the most influential area of women empowerment in Social, cultural and political

		contribution among women.
Studies related to infrastructural facilities in schools	Mangi pudy and Vankata (2010)	The study looks from the perspective of the principals and higher secondary school teachers, and finds that the availability of infrastructural facilities impacts the school enrollment.
		Gap: The study takes in to account only the school authorities as stakeholder, but parents are the important stakeholder and they are the decision makers to enroll their child in school, which is not taken in to consideration in the study.
Studies Related to Infrastructural Facilities In Schools	Boruah (2017)	The study says that parent's socio- economic condition of the parents and lack of community support is a reason for drop-out
		Gap: This study only focuses from the parents as stakeholders, other stakeholders such as schools, the teachers are also important stakeholder, which is not considered in the study.

Studies related to the teaching quality, professional development opportunities, and job satisfaction of teachers	Alvarez (2008); Lee (2013); Sekhar, Reddy and Nagarjuna (2014); Lawrence and Hanitha (2017); Baluyos (2019)	The studies reflect findings from the viewpoint of teachers in infrastructural facility, the opportunities for their growth and development and their job satisfaction. **Gap:** The above studies in thesedomains only cover the viewpoint of teachers,other stakeholders like school management, the governmental support and initiatives for teachers is not considered under the studies.
Studies related to the development of students	Zigarelli (1996) Preetham (2008), Annu S and Mishra S (2013)	The studies highlight the extracurricular activities planned and organized by the studentshave between participation of students in extracurricular activities and their academic progress. **Gap:** The studies only focus onextracurricular activities like organizing competitions, enhancing sports participation among students, but none of these studies describes the activities that can be taken up by the school to retain children from school dropout.

Studies related to the socio-economic status of Parents	Sirin (2005); Muhammed A and Akanle (2008); Memon G.R, et, al (2009); Huisman, Rani and Smit (2010); Chandra R and Azimuddin S (2013); Singh P and Chaudhary G (2015); Musangu M (2017)	All the studies highlight the impact of socio-economic status of parents and the academic performance and enrolment of students. **Gap:** All the studies undertaken only focus about the socio-economic status of parents and lacks consideration about aspects like occupation, educational qualification of parents which are also important factors towards the educational progress of children.
Studies related to educational status of parents	Bhatnagar and Sharma (1992); Kaur 2011; Vellymallay 2011; Qadri 2018	The studies reflect the educational status of parents, their involvement in education of children and the academic success of their children. **Gap:** The studies only consider theeducational status, the occupational status of the parents, which is one of the very vital factors in determining the enrolment of a child in school is not looked in to.

2.5 RATIONALE OF THE STUDY

The literature review points out the factors such as weaker socio-economic position of the family (Siddiqui-(1987), preference of giving importance to religious education rather than contemporary education (Mondal (1997) Chaturvedi (2004)), the patriarchal family structure of the family (Mondal (1997), Begum (1999), Hasan and Menon (2005), Waseem (2012)) ,fear of getting suitable marriage partner (Pande (2006)); prevalence of tradition beliefs and practices (Begum (1999), Chaturvedi (2009), Hasan and Menon (2005), Hussain (2018) Saha (2020)), parents prefer not to send their daughters in coeducational institutions (Ahmed (2016)).

The studies by (Bhatt, et, (2011)), depicts that irrespective of the governmental efforts to improve the status, Muslim women are still educationally deprived and because of educational deprivation, the Muslim women are weak in empowerment at all domains (Kundu and Chakraborty (2012), Salam (2019)). Women and girls from the Muslim community- one of the largest minorities in the nation according to Ministry of Minority Affairs are considered as a probable substance for the progress of the community (Jain 1988). In order to pave the way towards a comprehensive development of the nation, the ultimate importance should be given to provide developmental opportunities, which subsequently shall be beneficial in changing the attitudes and mindset of the community (Chaturvedi 2003)

The census data till 2011, it can be said that the number of school enrolment has increased over a period of time, but to keep the demand of the hour, not the quantity but the quality of education also has to be improved, this demands the active collaboration and associations of the various educational stakeholders - the previous highlights the reasons and not the role and contribution of stakeholders in education in totality.

Thereby, to have an improved vision and understanding of the subject of education among Muslim girls in India, in accordance with the role played by the associated stakeholders in the education detailed studies need to be undertaken at local level

Hence, precisely for these motives, the present study identifies the Muslim Managed Schools offering higher secondary education in Vadodara City and around, the principals of the Muslim managed schools, the higher secondary school teachers, Muslim girls studying in higher secondary classes, and the parents of Muslim girls studying in higher secondary classes as important stakeholders associated towards the education of Muslim girls.

2.6 IMPLICATIONS FOR THE STUDY

The problem of higher educational status among Muslims in India is a matter of concern since 1896. The subject is deeply studied, published from time to time by various academicians, the educationist and other optimistic thinkers of the community. The law makers are also not behind in addressing the grave concern, the government has also provided notable recommendations in five- year plans and setting up special committee- Sacchar committee- established with an intention to provide resolutions for the inclusive development of the largest minority- Muslims in the country.

Addressing towards the recommendations and inclusiveness of the Muslim community andspecifically for the Muslim girls, many initiatives are undertaken by the stakeholders such as establishing the schools, spreading the awareness on importance of higher education among Muslim girls. The literature review- the studies undertaken by **((Siddiqui 1987); (Mondal (1997); (Begum 1999); (Chaturvedi 2004); (Hasan and Menon 2005); (Pande 2006); (Waseem 2012))** highlighted various socio-economic factors responsible for lower higher educational status prevalent among Muslim community. On the other hand, the studies by ((Imtiyaz 2017), Saba et, al (2017)), focused that the change can only brought through the medium of education. The above-mentioned researches have implied the researcher to find out the educational status among Muslim girls studying in secondary as well as in higher secondary classes of Vadodara city. This gave an insight of fetching the data from the Muslim managed schools- the initiatives of the stakeholder of the community to address the issue of lower educational status of the community.

Further, the researches highlighting the contribution of the stakeholders like availability and accessibility of educational infrastructural facilities in school undertaken by **((Mangipudy& Venkata, (2010); Mylliemngap (2011); Nepal B (2016); Boruah (2017));** quality of teachers and related aspects highlighted by **(Alvarez (2008); Chaudhari N and Nagwanshee R (2019))**; opportunities for teacher's development by **(Zigarelli (1996); Lee (2013); Sekhar, Reddy and Nagarjuna (2014))**. The above-mentioned researches gave an implication to the researcher to find out the role of school-Muslim Managed schools of Vadodara city to explore their contribution as an educational stakeholder towards the education of Muslim girls.

Identifying another notable stakeholder – Parents of the Muslim girls studying in higher secondary classes, the studies by **(Sirin, (2005); Muhammed A and Akanle O (2008); Memon G.R, et, al (2009); Huisman, Rani, and Smits (2010); Chandra R and Azimuddin S (2013); Singh P and Chaudhary G (2015); Musangu M (2017))** mentioned the socio-economic status of the parents and its relevance with the educational status of children. The studies by (**Bhatnagar and Sharma (1992); Kaur (2011); Vellymallay (2011); Ogunshola & Adewale (2012); Qadri (2018)**) highlighted the relevance of educational qualification of parents with the education of children. Moreover, the studies by **(Saifullah and Mehmood, (2011); Faisal, (2014); Walter (2018); Moneva, Rozado and Sollano (2019))** focused on relation of occupational status of parents with the educational status of children. Similarly, the studies by **(Muthoni (2013); Giri (2014))** focused on the type of family and studies by **(Vijayalakshmi and Muniappan (2016); Prema (2016))** related involvement of parents in the education of their children. The above- mentioned researches gave an implication to explore the role of the parents of the Muslim girls studying in higher secondary classes of the schools selected for the study and to explore their home environment as well.

The studies by (**Baradei L and Amin K (2010); Nirmala K and Selvi P (2012); Kusumaningrum et, al (2017)**) focused the importance of community in the process of imparting quality education. This gave an implication to the researcher to find out the role of the Muslim community, towards the higher educational status among Muslim community.

Identifying the efforts of the law makers- the government, which plays an active role in taking up effective measures for the inclusion of Muslim community, through various scholarships programmes and schemes gave an implication to the researcher to find out the level of awareness among the community pertaining to the levied schemes and its beneficiaries.

Thus, considering the base of statistical data of Census 2011. AISHE 2018-19 data and the literature review mentioned implied the researcher to design the study.

CHAPTER-III

Research Methodology

General Idea of the Chapter:

Laying the objectives, the broad research questions for the study, as mentioned in chapter- I, a comprehensive study of the previous literature done in the context, situation, the factors,affecting the educational status among the Muslim community was undertaken. In addition,the stakeholders in the educational institutions and the roles played by them was exhaustively studied in Chapter-II, which weaved the thread of conceptualizing the study design.

This chapter discusses in detail the study statement, significance of the research methodology, the objectives of the study, the operational definitions of certain terms used for the study. The chapter also mentions about the tool used for data collection, the adoptionof sampling techniques, the process of validation of the research tools, the course of data collection, the techniques incorporated for the data analysis and the limitations encounteredby the researcher during the course of the study.

3.0 STATEMENT OF THE STUDY

Studying the role of various stakeholders involved in the education of Muslim girls and knowing the career aspirations of Muslim girls studying in higher secondary classes of Muslim managed schools in and around Vadodara.

3.1 OBJECTIVES OF THE STUDY

1) To study the number of Muslim girls in secondary and higher secondary classes in andaround Vadodara.

2) To explore the roles of the stakeholder in the education of Muslim girls.

   a. Exploring the role of School as an Educational Stakeholder

- b. Exploring the role of Parents of Muslim girls as an Educational Stakeholder.
- c. Exploring the role of Community as an Educational Stakeholder.
- d. Exploring the role of Government as an Educational Stakeholder.

3) To understand the home environment of Muslim girls.

4) To find out the career aspiration of Muslim girls.

3.2 EXPLANATION OF THE TERMS

1. **Stakeholders:** Stakeholder denotes to an individual who expresses one's curiosity anddemonstrate concern in an association. With reference to educational institutions, a stakeholder is an individual who directly or indirectly partakes conferred concentration towards the accomplishment of the objectives and the wellbeing of an educational institute.

2. **Career Aspirations:** A career aspiration characteristically mentions an enduring andcontinuing career vision that an individual desires to accomplishing future.

3. **Muslim Managed Schools**: According to the present study, the Muslim managed schools are those schools, which are managed by Muslim trusts/ organization in Vadodara and around.

4. **Higher Secondary Section:** In relevance with the current study, the Muslim girls enrolled with the Muslim managed schools in Standard XI and Standard XII refer to the higher secondary section.

5. **Home Environment:** In context with the present study, the home environment involves the socio-

economic position of the parents, the emotive support extended by parents, the facility of encouraging and motivating the educational process of Muslim girls.

6. **Career Aspirations:** The present study deals with the ambitions of the Muslim girls studying in higher secondary classes, after finishing their school education.

3.3 STUDY VARIABLES

The current study has Muslim Girls: Education as dependent variable, the schools, the parents of the Muslim girls as independent variable, the family income of the families of the Muslimgirls, the educational status among the parents of the Muslim girls as moderate variable, thetype of family and the number of children within the family of Muslim girls as moderate variable.

3.4 RESEARCH DESIGN

The research design for the current study is "Descriptive"- the descriptive studies are thosestudies, which describes the characteristics of a particular group. The main purpose of the descriptive research is to bring about the description of the particular group, community orthe society as it persists at the time of undertaking the research. The study is empirical, theinvestigator has collected the responses from the respondents in order to meet the study objectives.

3.5 UNIVERSE OF THE STUDY

The universe of the study comprises of Muslim managed schools in Vadodara city from allthe four directions: North, South, East and West and also some Muslim managed schools from rural areas such as Karjan, Savli, Bodeli, Chhotaudaipur and Dabhoi around Vadodaracity.

3.6 SELECTION OF SAMPLE FROM TOTAL POPULATION AND SAMPLE SIZE

a. Total number of populations from different respondents:

i. Total number of Principal = 21 (Equivalent to the number of Muslim managedschools in and around Vadodara city)

ii. Total number of Teachers = 452 (Number of teachers in the Muslim managedschools in and around Vadodara city)

iii. Total number of Muslim girls in higher secondary classes = 751(Number ofenrolments of Muslim girls in higher secondary classes)

iv. Total number of Muslim parents = 751 (Corresponding to the number ofenrolments of Muslim girls in higher secondary classes.

b. Sample size and Sampling technique

- The Sample size of the Muslim Managed school was 21- which was selected through stratified random sampling method

The following figure explains the diagrammatic representation of sampling techniques.

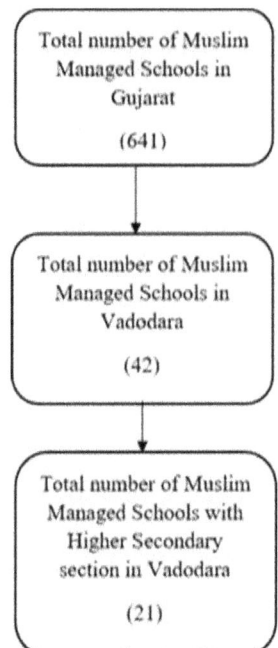

Figure3.0 Diagrammatic representation of Sampling technique

Purposive sampling was chosen, to gather the responses from 21 higher secondary schoolprincipals.

- Purposive sampling technique was used to fetch the data from 91 higher -secondary school teachers.
- To gather the data from the Muslim girls studying in higher secondary classes, purposive sampling technique was used on a sample size of 330.
- Convenient sampling and Snow ball technique was used to select the data onsample size of 100 parents of Muslim girls.

3.7 Overview of the Total Sampling

Sr. no	Particulars	Total Sample Size
1	Total Number of Muslim Managed School with Higher Secondary classes	21
2	Total Number of Principals as respondents	21
3	Total Number of Teachers of Higher secondary classes as respondents	91
4	Total Number of Muslim girls studying in Higher secondary classes of the selected schools	330
5	Total Number of Parents of Muslim girls studying in higher secondary classes of the selected schools	100
Total Sample size of the Study (Comprising of all the respondents of each category)		542

3.8 TOOLS USED FOR DATA COLLECTION

Separate tools were designed to gather response from all the categories of respondents:

I) Tools used for the principals of the Muslim managed school:

Questionnaire was used as a research tool, both in English as well as in regional - Gujarati language. The tool was categorized from Section A to Section F, comprising of general information of the respondent, information about the school, information about the teachers and the Supporting staff, views on quality in education, views on school effectiveness, views on education among Muslim girls and attitude of Muslim Parents towards girl's education. (Questionnaire for Principal in English enclosed in Appendix – III (A) (1))

(Questionnaire for Principal in Gujarati enclosed in Appendix – III (A) (1I))

II) Tools used for the Teachers of Higher Secondary classes of the Muslim managed school:

Questionnaire was used as tool, in both the languages English as well as in regional- Gujarati language. The questionnaire for the higher secondary teachers was categorized from SectionA to Section D including aspects like information of the Respondent, views on infrastructural facilities, views on teaching quality and teachers, views on education among Muslim girls and attitude of Muslim parents towards girl's education, views on support from community and Government in rendering quality education to Muslim girls.

III) Questionnaire for Teachers in English enclosed in Appendix-III(B)(I) Questionnaire for Teacher in Gujarati enclosed in Appendix-III(B)(II)

IV) Tools used for Muslim girls studying in Higher Secondary classes.

A semi structured interview schedule categorized from Section A to Section E was used asdata collection tool to gather responses from the Muslim girls studying in higher secondaryclasses on information of the respondent, views on Muslim girls on school infrastructure, views on quality teaching and teacher, views on home environment, views on educational status, parent's involvement & community support.

(Interview Schedule for Muslim girls in English enclosed in Appendix – III(C)

V) Tools used for Parents of Muslim girls studying in Higher Secondary classes.

In order to gather response from the parents of the Muslim girls, a semi structured interviewschedule was used for data collection, which was categorized from Section A to Section F,including information of the respondent, ratings on the parent's satisfaction with the infrastructural facilities of the schools, the teaching quality and the methods used in teachingby the teachers, the approach of the principal and the teachers, the curriculum, the guidanceto the parents from the teachers and the principal, opinion on the school infrastructural facilities, quality of teachers and teaching, views on the education of Muslim community/ government in the education of Muslim girls, views on the education of their girl child through open ended questions.

(Interview Schedule for Muslim girls in English enclosed in Appendix – III(D)

3.9 TOOL CREATION

With the help of the preliminary tools designed to undertake the pilot study from 10 schoolsof Vadodara, classifying 5 schools from the urban vicinity of the Vadodara city and 5 fromthe rural setting – Bhayli, Bill, Padra, Sangma and Chapad village, considering a sample size of 100 respondents.

The pilot testing of the tool was undertaken during June - July 2019, at the commencementof new academic year. The tools developed were analyzed on the following mentioned criteria's:

1. The flow of the questions in the tool

2. The over lapping questions within the tools
3. The nature of questions
4. The question refrained from speaking
5. The question "Not Answered"
6. The question Suggested
7. The question giving two meaning
8. The translation of the questions
9. The lead questions
10. The repetition of the question

Based on the data evaluation, so gathered during pilot testing and on the analysis of the tools on the above-mentioned criteria, the final construction of the tools was done.

3.10 TOOL VALIDATION

The research tools so designed were sent for the review and validation to the 7 experts. The feedbacks and the comments and their expertise is described in the following table: (List of Experts is enclosed in Appendix- D)

Table :3.10 Expert's feedback on research tool validation

Expert	Field of Expertise	Suggestions/ comments
A	Teacher from School	The expert commented as the topic was very relevant and pointed out certain grammatical errors in the tools.
B	Academics from School	No specific comments/ suggestion was given
C	Academics- Language	The expert commented as interesting study topic and pointed few grammatical errors in the statements of the tool and

		gave suggestions in the study objectives
D	Academics- Social work and Management	The study findings will be very informative and Suggested changes in the income range in the tool designed for Parents and Muslim Girls. Additionally, some minor changes in the statement of the question
E	Academics- Social work	The expert said that good objectives and findings will be very useful for policy matters and Muslim community. Moreover, the expert Suggested to avoid few questions for principals and teachers
F	Academics- Education and Psychology	The expert commented it to be a very comprehensive study. Suggested to avoid few questions for principals and teachers looking in to the objective of the study. Minor changes in the sentence for the study findings. Suggested to have five points rating scale instead of four. Reduce the number of questions
G	Academics- Education and Psychology	Suggested to avoid some questions and reduce the number of questions Minor grammatical errors Suggested for five points rating scale Suggested Three-point rating scale in Section -B a) in the tool for parents

3.11 SOURCE OF DATA COLLECTION

The data collected for the study purpose, is both through primary and secondary sources. Primary source was used for designing of research tools for all the categories of the respondents, by contacting school authorities, visiting schools on the decided time. During the given scheduled time by the school authority's interaction with Muslim girls of higher secondary classes was done, the researcher noted the contact address of the girls willing their parents to participate for the further home visits to the Muslim girls' residences and attending parents meeting arranged by the school authorities. The information gathered by Millat Educational directory for the contact details and the address of the schools was the secondary information used for the study.

3.12 PROCESS OF DATA COLLECTION

a. DATA COLLECTION FROM THE SCHOOLS

The researcher through telephonic appointments, approached the school principals. On the schedule day of the visit in a particular school, formal meeting was undertaken with the head of the schools and the higher secondary teachers of the selected school, wherein the objectives, the purpose of the study was informed to them and then the questionnaire as a research tool designed separately for the principal and the higher secondary teachers was disseminated. The response of the questionnaire from the head of the schools and the higher secondary teachers, in some cases- as it took the whole day in interviewing the girls, the teachers and the principals were able to respond and return the filled- up questionnaires on the same day, whereas some of them requested to collect it some other day, and in case of distant areas, the filled in questionnaire was returned digitally. Some principals returned the questionnaire the same day, during the presence of the researcher in the school premises, whereas, some of them responded through email.

Correspondingly, on the scheduled day of the visit, Muslim girls studying in XI and XII classes, and those willing to participate in the study process, were interviewed in the school premises and during the school hours only. While interviewing the girls, the researcher had recorded their personal residential address and the contact details of those girls who were willing to participate the researcher at their residence for the purpose of data collection from their parents.

b. DATA COLLECTION FROM THE PARENTS

Based on the contact information collected during interviews of Muslim girls, the appropriate timings and the date was scheduled with the parents of the Muslim girls at their residence, based on the contact details, the parents were telephonically consulted to confirm their availability and the suitable timings for the interview. Hence, on the scheduled day of the home visit, with a prior phone call to confirm about the availability, interviews with parents were undertaken and thus 38 home visits were undertaken by the researcher

While for the remaining respondents, the school had permitted to interview the parents during the Parent Teacher's Meeting held in the school premises, hence the interviews were undertaken with parents ready to participate after the scheduled meetings by the school authorities.

3.13 PROBLEMS FACED DURING DATA COLLECTION

While interviewing Muslim girls, because of the introvert nature of some girl's student, it was difficult to gather their views openly, as they did not feel comfortable sharing their home background. On questioning the career aspiration of the Muslim girls, it was noted that though the interviews were undertaken turn by turn of each girl, the response on the career aspiration were repeatedly shared in common by some of the Muslim girls as their peers.

During the home visits, mostly the researcher interacted with the mother – as the father didnot interacted with the female researcher. Moreover, in the presence of other family members,the responses of the mother of the Muslim girls were answered by other family members, while in some cases the mothers confirmed with other family members about the information shared specifically the family income. Hence the information was not openly shared with the researcher and was difficult to take the correct views.

3.14 DATA ANALYSIS

The data so collected was systematically analyzed according to the study objectives. Frequency table, bivariate table, the cross-section table, statistically one-way ANOVA test wasdone using the IBM SPSS statistic 21 and Microsoft Excel was used to analyze the quantitative data. The qualitative data – of open-ended question was analyzed using ContentAnalysis.

3.15 DE LIMITATION OF THE STUDY

1. The study is conducted in a sample size of 21 Muslim managed schools, in and around Vadodara city, hence the data cannot be generalized.
2. The responses from the Muslim girls studying in higher secondary classes is also selected from the limited sample size from the Vadodara city and around, hence the data also cannot be generalized as well as there could be variations in terms of geographical locality and the area of residence.

3.16 LIMITATION OF THE STUDY

1. The study bears the limitations of the tool used for the study purpose, the questionnaire was used for the principal and teachers, hence there was no direct conversation with the school authorities.
2. Some of the responses from the girls' students were having commonality which was influenced by their peer responses.
3. While doing Home Visits to collect the data from the parents as respondents, the responses were not very accurate as, mostly the mothers were not very open in sharing their opinions with the researcher.
4. Some general lessons are derived from the study, which is limited to the selected sample size only, which cannot be commonly generalized to similar such educational institutions.

Findings, Conclusions and Suggestions

General Idea of the Chapter: On the basis of data analysis and interpretation of the data collected for the study purpose, this chapter reveals the major findings of the study, precisely arranged as per the study objective. Based on the findings the present chapter draws the conclusions as well as the suggestions of the study

(Section-A)- Findings related to the study background: This section of the study findings is related with the background study findings such as the school profiles, the profile of the respondents.

Table:5.0 Profile of the Muslim managed schools as study background

Particulars	Findings
Inception	1980's
Type of School	Private
Medium of Instruction	Gujarati
Affiliation	Gujarat Secondary and Higher Secondary Education Board
School demography	Co-education
Streams offered in HSC	Commerce
Gender wise Teacher's distribution	More Female teachers

About the Profile of the School: From the table 5.0, the data reveals that majority of the Muslim Managed schools chosen for the study were private schools who had their inceptionduring 1980's, was offering Gujarati language as a medium of instruction and its association with Gujarat Secondary and Higher Secondary Education board. Widely, the schools were co-education school and was offering the commerce stream in higher secondary classes. Almost all the schools had more female teachers than male teacher.

Table :5.0.1 Demographic profile of the respondents as background information of the study

Particulars	Principals			Teachers	Girls		Parents	
Age Group	41-50			31-40	15-17		31-40	
Educational qualification	B. Ed			B. Ed	From and class	11th 12th	F	M
							Sec	Pri
Total Work Experience	More than 10 years			More than 10 years	NA		NA	
Work experience as principal/ in current school	More years	than	5	1-5 years	NA		NA	
Occupation of Father	NA			NA	NA		Business and Daily wage earner	
Occupation of Mother	NA			NA	NA		Home Makers	
Type of Family	NA			NA	Nuclear		NA	
Monthly Income	NA			NA	Less than 10,000		10,001- 20,0001	

Demographic profile of Principals: From the table 5.0.1, the data indicates that majority of the principals were belonging to the age group of 41-50 years, having B.Ed. as their educational qualification and work experience of more than 10 years. Majority of the principals were serving as principal for more than 5 years.

This indicates that majority of the principals were qualified and possessed good academic experience.

Demographic profile of Higher Secondary School Teachers: The data reveals that majority of the higher secondary school teachers from the Muslim managed schools chosen for the study, were from the age group of 31-40 years, possessing B.Ed. as their educational qualification, with more than 10 years of working experience and their association of 1-5 years with the schools chosen for the study.

This specifies that widely the teachers in the schools chosen were qualified and owned good academic experience.

Demographic profile of Muslim girls: Conveniently, the study chose Muslim girls studying in standard XI and XI in the age group of 15-17 years. Majority of the girls belonged to nuclear families possessing the monthly income of less than 10,000 ₹.

This shows that majority of the girls were from the lower income families.

Demographic profile of Parents of Muslim girls: Through convenient and snowball technique, majority of parents were in the age group of 31-40 years, majority of fathers were educated till secondary classes, whereas majority of the mothers were educated till primary classes. Looking in to the occupation, majority of the fathers were either having small scale business, and number of girls whose fathers were daily wage earners were also more. Comparatively, the majority of mothers were home makers.

The families that fall within the income level of 10,001-20,000 Rs were also more.

The findings shows that there was lack of higher education among both the parents of the Muslim girls. Further, comparison indicates that the education level among mothers is lower than the fathers. The occupation status also indicates that majority of the parents were managing their own business or were daily wage earners whereas mothers were the home makers. Therefore, it can be said that because of the lower educational status among the parents, there is less participation of parents towards the workforce and, further comparing the participation of male and females, females are more home makers.

(Section-B) - Findings related to the elementary information of the study: This section of the study findings is related with the elementary study information such as the Gender equality in education by the Muslim community, the enrolment rate, the drop-out rate, the growth rate of Muslim girls, availability of infrastructural facilities within the schools as specified in the study objective No- 2. This section also highlights the findings for lower higher education among Muslim girls.

Table: 5.1.1 Enrolment and drop-out data of Muslim girls from secondary to higher secondary classes as elementary study information.

Particulars	Findings
Gender Equality in education	Views form Parents
	62%- No gender discrimination
	38%- More preference to boy's education
Findings	There is no gender discrimination in terms of education

Class Strength of Muslim girls in Secondary classes (2017-2018) (2018-2019)	50-100
Class Strength of Muslim girls in higher Secondary classes (2017-2018) (2018-2019	Less than 50
Findings of Comparison between secondary and H.SC classes	It can be noted that the drop-out rate is higher in higher secondary classes. Precisely those studying in government schools drop-out earlier than those girls studying in the aided and the private schools
Implications:	So, it can be implied that rate of drop out girls in higher education is more.
Reasons for the drop-out rate	76.19% - Principals accounted Lack of awareness on importance of education among the Muslim community, as one of major reason for high drop-out of girls from higher secondary classes. 53.84% - Teachers stated conservative mindset of parents and lack of support from the family members for higher education is a reason for high drop-out rate of girls from higher secondary classes.

Findings	Majority of the principals as well as the teachers connectedthe lack of awareness among the Muslim parents/ community as the major responsible factor for the drop-out of Muslim girls from the schools, due to which less priorityand less support is provided to girls for higher education.
Implications	Lack of awareness and lack of sensitization towards the education of girls among the community, there is a highdrop-out rates among the girls from higher secondary classes.

About the Enrolment of Muslim Girls in Schools: Majority of the enrolment of Muslim girls were found in private schools. The class strength of Muslim girls in secondary classeswas 50-100, and it reduced to less than 50 in higher secondary classes. This shows that the drop-out rates of Muslim girls are higher in higher secondary classes.

Analyzing the data, it can be said that though, they say that there is no gender inequality interms of education, however, the drop- out rates of Muslim girls from higher secondary classes, depicts that there is gender inequality, specifically for higher education of Muslim girls. Therefore, it can be said that the schools are been established, planned and organized to improve the educational status of the community, yet unable to control the drop- out ratesof girls especially from higher education classes.

Connecting "Strategic drift" concept with establishment of schools, it can be said that the schools have been established looking in to the cultural factors and historical data of lower educational status among Muslim girls, but the outcome is not very successful in coming their pace with the present social, economic, and educational situation of the country.

Table: 5.1.2 Findings of Infrastructural facilities in schools and itsimpact on school enrolment as elementary study information

Views of girls on	Findings					
Classroom Facilities	Satisfied-		Moderately satisfied -		Needs Improvement	
	Govt & aided schools	45.75%	Private schools	36.36 %	Govt, Private & Aided	17.87%:
	Total	45.75%	Total	36.36%	Total	17.87%
Implications	It can be implied that the private schools are lacking the basicessential facilities in classrooms.					
Library facilities	Using Sometimes		Not Using		No library	
	Private	27.57%	Govt	14.51%	Private	20%
	Aided	11.51%	Aided	9.39%	Govt	5.45%
	Govt	4.84%	Private	6.66%		
	Total	43.92%	Total	30.56%	Total	25.45%
Implications	It can be implied that the Government, and aided schools werehaving library facility in the school, whereas some private schools did not have library facility.					
Computer lab/ Science lab	During Period		Not Using		No Labs	
	Private	24.84%	Private	23.33%	Private	6.06%
	Aided	11.51%	Aided	9.39%		
	Govt	3.03%	Govt	21.81%		
	Total	39.38%	Total	54.53%	Total	6.06

Implications	Majority of the girls are not using labs. It can be implied that all the government and aided schools are having the lab facilities, and some private schools does not have the lab facilities. Thus, Private schools are lacking in the adequate infrastructural facilities.					
Indoor/ outdoor sports facilities	During Period		Not Using		No Labs	
	Private	23.333%	Private	2.42%	Private	22.72%
	Aided	13.03%	Aided	16.06%		
	Govt	22.42%	Govt			
	Total	58.78%	Total	18.48%	Total	22.72%
Implications	It can be inferred that the girls show less interest towards participation in sports activities. Thus, Private schools are lacking in the suitable sports facilities, so there are less opportunities for physical growth and development of students.					
Washroom facilities	Using Sometimes		Using Regularly		Not Using:	
	Private and government	38.78%-	Private	11.51%-	Private	22.12%
	Aided	13.93%-	Aided	1.21%	Aided	5.75%
			Govt	5.15%	Govt	1.51%
	Total	52.71%	Total	17.87%	Total:	29.38
Implications	It can be implied that the private schools lack proper cleanliness of washroom facilities.					
Canteen Facilities	No Canteen		Not using			
	Private	41.21%-	Private	11.21%		
	Aided	18.18%	Aided & Govt	4.54%-		
	Govt	24.84%				
	Total	84.23%	Total	15.75%		
Implications	It can be inferred from the explicit data, that the girls are not using the canteen, they prefer to go back their homes as most of the girls are enrolled in school in and around their residential areas.					
Assembly Hall	No Hall		Need Based			
	Private	41.21%	Private	13.03%		

			Aided	20.9%		
	Govt	0.9%-	Govt	23.93%-		
	Total	42.11%	Total	57.86%		

Implications	It can be inferred that the assembly halls are available in government and aided schools, which are used as per need only. Private schools did not have the provision of assembly hall.

Rest Rooms	No Rest Room		Need Based			
	Private	41.21%	Private & Govt	26.96-		
			Aided	20.9%-		
	Govt	10.69%				
	Total	51.9	Total:	47.86		

Implications	It can be said that majority of the schools do not have the rest room facility for girls.

Washing Area	Required		Available		Not needed	
	Private	29.69%\	Private	13.03%	Private	11.51%
	Aided &Govt	4.24 %	Aided	20.9%		
			Govt	18.18%	Govt	2.42%
	Total	33.93	Total:	52.11	Total	13.93

Implications	It can be inferred that the school management are also taking care of their religious prayers and the essential facilities required in the school premises

Prayerroom	Required		Available		Not needed	
	Private	24.24%	Private	57.57%	Private	11.51%
			Aided & Govt		Aided	
	Govt	4.24%			Govt	2.42%-
	Total	28.48	Total:	57.57	Total:	13.93

Implications	Majority of the schools do provide the other required facilities to Muslim students along with the basic infrastructural facilities in schools.			
	Hence it can also be said that the parents of the Muslim girls look in to the provision of such facilities in school while enrolling their daughters in schools.			
Impact of Infrastructural facilities on enrolment of Muslim girls in Schools				
From the perspective of Principal	Agreed that it has its impact	76.19%	Do not have its impact	23.80%
From the Perspective of Teachers	Agreed that it has its impact	79.12%	Impact to some extent	18.68%
			Can't Say	2.19%
Findings	Obvious data that the availability of good infrastructural facilities in school is a decision-making factor for parents as well as girls studying to get themselves enrolled in good schools with adequate infrastructural facilities.			
Implications	**From the School authorities**: It can be said that, though 76.19% of principals and 79.12% of teachers agree that the infrastructural facilities have impact over the enrolment of girls, yet the schools are lacking in strategic as well as succession planning to plan for the upgradation of the required facilities in the schools, specifically the private schools, since they have access to as well as have autonomy in decision making.			
	From the Parents: It can be inferred that the parents do not give more attention to the availability of good infrastructural facilities, rather prefer sending their daughters in the schools which is nearby the residential area.			
Future Plan on Infrastructural Development				
From the perspective of Principal	12.08%- Focused on Technological Upgradation			
	7.69%- Focused on Infrastructural development			
	3.29%- They do not have autonomy and power to take decisions 76.94%- Not responded			
Findings	Private schools are lacking in providing essential facilities in classrooms, library, computer labs/ science labs, indoor/ outdoor sports facilities and the principals are planning to have such facilities for future.			

Implications	Hence it can be Implied that the private schools have the autonomy to make their decisions pertaining to the developmental plans, yet there is lack of strategic management for the development of the students as well as the staff, among the private school.
	Whereas in government and aided schools totally rely on the availability and budgets from the government

Conclusions: Availability and Significance of the Infrastructural facilities inschool:

Pertaining to the availability of Infrastructural facilities in school, the private schools have all the authorities and have the autonomy in taking decisions pertaining to the upgradation of basic as well as educational infrastructural facilities within the school premises, yet the schools covered under the study are lacking in providing such basic educational as well as infrastructural facilities in schools.

Connecting the Human Capital Theory, it can be said that the "Human Resource" Investment is found lacking by these schools in terms of providing the adequate classroom as well as basic educational infrastructural facilities in school.

Suggestions:

Based on the findings and conclusions related to the availability and accessibility of infrastructural facilities, it can be suggested that the private Muslim managed schools covered under the study, should develop "Student centric" approach for providing the needed educational infrastructural facilities for the progress, development of the students and special facilities for girls students such as a provision of hygienic washroom and cleanliness facilities, and rest rooms for the students studying in the schools as one the "Schools" are considered as one of the important stakeholder performing the role of facilitator in rendering quality education

Relating "Power/ Interest Matrix". The matrix helps in thinking through stakeholderinfluences on the development of strategy, thus the school administrators need to focus on the required needs for the development and upgradation using all the power and autonomy they have in decision making

Table: 5.1.3 Educational Status among Muslim Girls in schools andattitude towards higher education as elementary study information

Quantitative data analysis	
Class Performance Of Muslimgirls	From the perspective of teachers: 41.75%- Academic performance is good 25.27%- Need encouragement/ motivation
Findings	Majority of the teachers finds that the girls are really doing goodin academics in higher secondary classes.
Implications	It can be implied from the data that the because of lack of awareness, lack of parent's education, financial constraints in the family and social and religious restrictions, though they are having good class performance, yet they are unable to go for higher education
Qualitative data analysis	
Findings	The data reveals that that the teachers are really making efforts to retainthe girls in school by implementing various ways of guidance and counselling to retain the students in the class.
Reasons oflower enrolment of Muslim girls In highereducation	62.63%- Lack of family support/ a smaller number of universities for girls 41.75%- Less priority of girl's education/ conservative mindset of the community
Findings	The data shows that because of the lack of family support and a smaller number of universities only for girls, girls are not allowed for highereducation.

Implications	Hence, it can be implied that because of safety issues, and fear of wrong peer influence, parents do not prefer to send their daughters in a co- education university, and because of lack of such universities, they do not allow girls for higher education

Conclusion: The data on the higher educational status among Muslim girls reveals that there is high drop-out rate of Muslim girls in standard XI and XII classes, because of lack of education, lack of awareness, financial crunches within the family, there is lack of sensitization towards education, the outcome of which is less enrolment of girls in highereducation, which subsequently impacts their contribution in the social development as well as the economic contribution of the nation

Suggestions: Based on the data, it can be suggested an "Investment" has to be made in spreading awareness pertaining to the importance of education among the community. This can be done through strategic management and active collaboration of all the key stakeholders such as the schools, the educationist, the social workers and other educatedmembers of the community. The spreading and disseminating of the information and

investment made in such domain will bring about return in the positive way in the longrun.

(Section-C)- Findings related to the Direct Impact of Schools towards the education of Muslim girls: This section of the study indicates the direct impact of schooling on the education of Muslim girls ; such as the training of teachers , the innovative pedagogies usedby the teachers in their classroom teaching, the impact of teachers counselling in retention of Muslim girls in higher secondary classes, the impact of initiatives taken by schools for the social and psychological development of students; the parental factors like the education, the occupation, the involvement of parents in the education of girls, the home environment of the girls.

Table:5.2.1 Teachers training and teaching quality of teachers as direct impact of schools

Training of Teachers	From the Perspective of Principals: (Quantitative) 61.9%-personal and professional growth of teachers such as communication skills, personality development (Yearly Basis) 38.09% said that they want to give training for the technological upgradation of teachers. (Future planning)
Findings	Majority of the Principals said that the schools are planning, organizing as well as conducting the training session for the teaching staff on the development of soft skills.
Implications	From the data, it can be implied that the schools lack in organizing a need-based training programme, the training programmes are organized once a year by the school management in all the type of school- private, Government and aided. Hence the "investment" in the human resources specifically reflected by Human Capital Theory is less and also the provision of "equal opportunities" reflected in person centered approach is also inevitable practiced in the schools covered under the study.
Impact of teacher's Counselling on retention of Muslim girls in higher secondary classes	70.32% yes it helps in retention (Through Counselling to parents/girls and sometimes home visits) 23.07%- Partially was able to retain (Through Counselling to parents/ girls and sometimes home visits) 6.59%- No they were not successful

Findings	From the data it can be said that the teachers are really making efforts to retain the girls in school by adopting various measures as a part of their ethical responsibility, however the investment done is not giving the expected outcome.
Implications	From the data it can be said that girls are able to complete their highersecondary classes and are not pursuing higher education, hence it can be pointed that the higher education among Muslim girls is very less

Qualitative data analysis from the perspective of students

Teaching Quality and use of innovative pedagogiesin teaching	From the obvious data that in majority of the schools, whether private, government or aided, the teachers are having good subject knowledge and are usingtextbooks in their daily teaching, the use of audio-visual aids in teaching is less.	Hence it can be implied that because of lack of audio- visual aids in classrooms, the teachers are using textbooks and supplement the concepts through examples.

Conclusion: Teacher's Training

Pertaining to the Training of Teachers: Training comprise an essential part in an educational institution. The ANOVA Single factor test conducted for the study also reveals that the teachers training, pedagogy used and implemented, and availability of infrastructural facilities have a strong impact on the student's development, From the data, it can be said that the training programmes are planned, organized and implemented by the government schools and the aided schools, yet the private schoolslag behind in conducting need-based training for the teachers. Relating the Human Relation approach, the teachers as well as the students should be provided with the equal opportunities for their own progress and development, to deliver the best outcome, is found deficient in the private Muslim Management schools selected under the study.

Suggestions:

The school authorities through its proper "Investment" in planning for resources shouldensure availability and accessibility of educational infrastructural facilities such as projectors, audio- visual system within the classroom and should ensure its usage whichshall bring subject clarity and interest among the students which subsequently will develop interest towards studies.

Table 5.2.2: Analysis of initiatives taken for students for academic, social andpsychological development as direct impact over the educational status of Muslim girls

Quantitative data analysis	
Activities for Academic developmentof students	38.09%- Organizing competition 33.33%- Classes for academically weak students 28.57%- only academics/ no extra activities
Findings	Majority of the schools are organizing elocution, essay writing, science exhibition, for the development of cognitive, innovative, leadership qualities among the students by planning and organizing such activities, subsequently encouraging active participation for further enhancement of skills.
Implications:	It can be inferred from the data, that the schools are really taking active actions by planning and organizing the competitions for theacademic development of students.
Social & Psychological developmentof students	28.57%- Conducting Expert's session, counselling by teachers (Govt,private and aided) 23.80%- Encouraging for co- curricular activities (Private and aided)19.04% - only academics/ no extra activities (Govt Schools)

Findings	It can be said from the data, that there are initiatives planned and undertaken for the development of the students by the school authorities as well as teachers are also performing the roles of the facilitator by taking counselling session so as to retain the students in higher secondary classes as well as motivating them for higher studies.
Implications	Connecting the development aspects of both the teachers as well as the students, it can be implied that the private schools lack in the strategic management in providing the developmental opportunities to the teaching staff, whereas the government schools exhibit lacunain undertaking the activities for the development of students. Hence, there is a lack of Comprehensive management aspects in the schools which look in to overall development of all the associated stakeholder.

Qualitative data analysis from the perspective of students

Students Development	Majority of the schools and the teachers do take care and provides encouragement and motivation to girls for higherstudies as well as give counselling to parents, and also organize aid them by providing special classes, waiving off fees and providing stationeries to theneedy students	It can be implied that the majority of the school's support students through resources, but proper career guidance and counselling by experts is not stressed on.

Conclusion:

Connecting the return of Investment (ROI) concept with the inputs undertaken for the academic, social as well as social and psychological development of students by the schools as well as the teachers with an attempt to increase and higher educational rate among Muslim girls, it can be concluded that the investment done by the schools by organizing remedial classes, counselling by teachers, various activities and competitions organized by the schools is not giving expected returns on the investmentdone.

Suggestions on Student's Academic, social and psychological development:

Along with focus of organizing competition and remedial classes for academicallyweak students, there should also be training and orientation for the essential skills suchas leadership, problem solving and Interpersonal skills which subsequently will helpthem in future prospects as well.

More orientation, lecture and workshops shall be organized by the school authorities which provides them information about the importance of education, the success stories of the girls of the Muslim community who have excelled in their field of profession, organizing career and guidance workshops, right from the time of their transition from secondary to higher secondary classes i.e from standard X.

Table:5.2.3 Parental factors as direct impact over the educational status of Muslim girls.

Quantitative data analysis on various school aspects - Frequency	
Age and Gender ofthe parents	Majority of Fathers are from the age group of 41-50 years(n=51) And Majority of Mothers are from the age group of 31- 40years (n= 36)

Occupation of the parents	Majority of the Fathers are owning small business or are daily wage earners (n=29) such as running a garage, a provision or a stationery shop/ selling dairy products, are suppliers to automobile / or owning the garment shop, vegetable vendors, auto-rickshaw drivers, working as helper in some other shops. Majority of the mothers are the home makers (n=34)
Findings	The data indicates that majority of the mothers are from the age group of 31-40 years, and are only performing their roles in their homes.
Implications	From the data, the age difference among both the parents can be indicated, mothers at the age of 31-40 years are having their daughters of 15-17 years, hence the inferential says that majority of mothers were married early. Because of lack of education, since mothers were married early, they all accepted the household responsibility and hence they are not making any contribution towards the economic development of the nation.
Parents satisfaction with Infrastructural facilities at schools and related aspects	Satisfied 31%- Govt, 25% - private, 15% aided	Needs Improvement 11% - private, 4% - aided 1% - govt school-
	The mean and correlation of parent's satisfaction with the infrastructural facilities in the school premises, and other aspects like implementation of the curriculum, approach of teachers and principals demonstrated negative correlation	
Findings	Negative correlation was observed between the parents as an influencer and other related aspects with the school. They are not concerned about the infrastructural facilities, neither are demanding,

Implications	It can be said that because of lack of education among parents, andless involvement of parents in the education of girls, they are contended to the infrastructural facilities as well as the quality in teaching by the schools, and for them the quality in teaching is nota matter of concern, rather prefer to send their daughters in schools which is near their residential areas.
Qualitative data analysis on various school aspects - Content Analysis	
Reasons for Enrolment of Daughters in Muslim Managed schools	46%- A school with good infrastructural facilities and Muslimculture 41%- A Muslim cultured school, nearby residence and a low budget school 13% was derived where parents said that they prefer to send theirdaughters to schools which are near the residential areas.
Findings	Parents give less preference towards the availability of good infrastructural facilities in school and the quality education, butrather prefer to send their daughters in schools which is nearbytheir residential areas and the schools which has Muslim culture in terms of their Uniforms, allowed to do prayers on time etc.
Implications	Parents are more concerned about the safety and they have fear ofwrong peer influence, and so they prefer to send to the schools nearby their residence only. This shows that there is impact of cultural influence on takingdecision pertaining to the enrolment of their daughters in schools.
Parents views on Quality in Teaching	62%- Teachers are well acquainted, approachable and give clarity29%- Teachers are not co-operative.

	9%-parents said that the teachers are only using the textbooks forteaching, innovative pedagogies need to be used by the teachers
Findings	Majority of the parents were satisfied with the quality in educationrendered by teachers in schools,
Implications	Because of the lack of education and less involvement of parents in the education of girls, they are contended to the infrastructural facilities as well as the quality in teaching by the schools, and for them the quality in teaching is not a matter of concern.
Parents views on guidance to Students by teachers	49%- Teachers provides guidance 28%- Extra classes are arranged by teachers23%- No guidance and counselling
Findings	Majority of the schools' teachers are providing guidance support toboth the parents as well to their parents, especially when they come to schools during the result timings
Implications	Schools are taking active efforts to promote higher education among girls but because of the lack of education and conservativemindset of the parents and the community, the girls are not permitted for higher education.
Impact of Schooling on Socialand Psychological development of students	54%-daughters realize the importance of higher education and theyare aspiring for higher education, have gained self-confidence, hasbecome mature in their disposition 52%- their daughters have developed understanding and are maturein their behaviors 30%- Monitor their daughters- they are in wrong peer influence
Findings	Majority of the parents shared optimistic development of theirstudent due to their schooling.

Implications	Analyzing the parents' perspective, it can be implied that Return on investment over their daughter's education is sustaining to the parents
Parents occupation and their support for higher education	Occupation of the parents is a very detrimental factor in the education of the daughters, majority of the fathers who were in service sector (n=15) realized the importance of education and spoke that they will support their daughter's education. Majority of mothers were the homemakers, they also said that they will support their daughters for higher education
Views on girl's safety in schools	53%-Management takes active steps in maintain safety 38%- Entry/ Exit of the outsiders have to be monitored 9%- Satisfied with safety, but emphasized towards female counsellor
Findings	Girl's safety is taken care of in all the schools
Implications	Since the schools are situated amidst the residential areas, there are no strict rules and regulations pertaining to the entry of the outsiders as well as the parents also walk in at any point of time which needs to be worked on by the school management. There has to be proper utilization of authority/ power by the school authorities which should prevent entry and exit of frequent visitors within the school premises.
Acceptance of parent's suggestion	57%- Management accepts and implements the suggestion 23%-No PTM is held 11%- Do not participate in meetings 9%- Suggestions are taken but not implemented
Findings	In majority of the Muslim managed school Parent Teacher' sMeetings are organized and the suggestions shared by the parents during meetings is well taken in to consideration and are implemented as well

Implications	It can be implied that those parents who really do not pay much attention towards the education of their daughters said that they do not participate in the meetings organized by the school. Relating to the stakeholder, it can be said that the schools are taking parents suggestions as the external stakeholder for further, improvements, developments needed in the school.
Findings	Based on the data, it can be said that there is lack of education among both the parents, which is subsequently evident from their contribution in the employment sector. Due to lack of awareness and less importance driven towards girls' education, parents prefer to enroll their daughters in the schools which is nearby the residential areas, accessibility of infrastructuralfacility is of no importance to them. Moreover, tit was observed that they were satisfied with the overall development of their children. Occupation of the parents is one of the decisive factors, Fathers who were in the service sector, were involved in the education of their daughters and were willing to support their daughters, Whereas, majority of mothers were home makers, yet they wantedto support their daughters for their higher education, but they did not had autonomy in decision making.
Implications	It can be implied that various factors such as education of parents, their occupation, their support and involvement towards the education of their daughters is influencing factor for the highereducation of girls. Hence, analyzing parents as stakeholder, it can be said that there isa gap in the power matrix, they have the power and autonomy, yetthey are unable to utilize their power in appropriate manner, because of the cultural influence

Qualitative data analysis on educational status among Muslims- ContentAnalysis	
Reasons of lowerhigher educational status among Muslim girls	43% - responded Financial Constraints and parental restriction 31% -Safety issue and lack of proper guidance, 19% conservativemindset of the community. 7%- Religious obligations
Findings	Majority of the parents said that the Muslim girls are not sent forhigher education, and considers financial constraints and parentalrestrictions as the main reasons for hindering the higher educational status among Muslim
Implications	It can be said that due to lack of education, parents are mostly in small business and moreover, because of the conservativemindset of the parents and the community, parents impose restrictions like wearing Hijab/ Burkha, not permitting their daughters to study in co-education universities, which results in lower enrolment of Muslim girls in higher education. Analyzing, the reasons it can be said that there are environmental and cultural influences that obstructs the stakeholders like schools, resulting in lower educational status.
Reason for supporting higher education for their daughters.	31%- (Mothers) and 24% (Fathers) for their own better future 9%- (Mothers) and 11 % of (Fathers) Respectable position in thecommunity 7% (Mothers) and 3% of (Fathers) not allowed to go for higherstudies
Findings	Majority of the mothers are willing to support the higher educationof their daughters.

Implication	Mothers want their daughters to be self-reliant, confident, but majority of them are not the decision makers of the family, so they were not confident enough to say that they will strongly support for higher education of their daughters. Relating the power matrix, the lack of decision-making power is one another factor obstructing because of patriarchal dominance in the culture.
Findings	Larger segment of the populations felt that there is a need to spread awareness among the community pertaining to the relevance and importance of education.
Implications	It needs to have joint collaboration among all the stakeholders, the school, the social workers, the non-government organizations, the voluntary organizations, the educationist of the community, with an intention to give access to equal opportunities for the development of the individual, society and the nation.
Suggestions	It can be suggested that, since parents becomes an important stakeholder and their decision is very important factor, hence it is important to get their support and so, there should be awareness created by active collaboration of all the stakeholders such as schools, the social worker, the educationist. Because of lack of awareness among the community, the parents experience community pressure for not permitting daughters for higher education, hence the awareness on importance of education has to be created among the community.

Table:5.2.4 Home environment as the direct impact over the educationalstatus among Muslim girls

Qualitative data analysis of home environment - Content Analysis	
Particulars	Findings
Age of Parents	Majority of mother's, in the age group of 31-40 years, whereas majority of the parents both mother and father werein the age group of 41-50 years.
Occupation and Educationof Fathers	Higher education among Muslim males is less and majority ofthem are having business as their occupation
Occupation and Educationof Mothers	Participation of Muslim females in work force is very lessas only 3.33% of Muslim females are in to the service.
Type of Family and Monthly Income	Muslim girls came from a nuclear family background, with majority of them having monthly income to be less than 10,000 ₹
Monthly Income andenrollment in schools	Majority of girls have their family monthly income less than10,000₹, yet they are enrolled with private Muslim managedschools.
Guidance, Monitoring and Academic Help	Majorly mothers are having their education till primary classes, they are not able to help in academics of their children, however,they keep track about the related aspects such as punctuality, instruction and constant reminders to do well and to study is doneby mothers.
Participation of Parents inParent Teachers Meetings	Because of lack of education, there is less preference given towards the education of girls and hence parental involvement is found to be less among the respondents.

Autonomy to girls in going to school/coaching classes	Majority of the girls are allowed to go independently to school /coaching classes.
Responsibility of Domestic chores/ Compulsions/ freedom to take decisions	There is no autonomy/ freedom given to girls in terms of taking decision pertaining to the educational as well as recreational needs, they have compulsions in terms of their attire. So, it can be inferred from the implicit data that because of such restrictions imposed on the girls, they lack self-confidence, unable to partake in the workforce and also are unable to achieve their aspirations
Implications	Because of lack of education among the parents, and lower family income among the families and due to safety issues, they are enrolling their daughters which are nearby the residential areas. Lack of education among parents also prevents them to get involved in to the education of their children. Along with the social and economic factors, they are also very much under cultural influence, which restricts their mobility, which subsequently is impacting on their decision of having professional careers. The imposition of restrictions does not lead to comprehensive professional development and hence they are unable to partake in the employment sector. Overall, which has its impact on the standard of living and have its deep impact on social, economic and political development of the community and the nation at large.

Suggestions	Persistent awareness pertaining to the importance of education is needed. The school authorities who are the primary stakeholders in the educational institutions should plan and implement the seminars, the lectures, the talks which caters the issues relating to importance of education. Special guidance and counselling sessions can be organized. The active collaboration of all the stakeholders is needed to address the issue of lack of higher education among Muslim girls.

Table:5.2.5 Analysis of career aspiration of girls as a direct impact of the educational status among Muslim girls

Quantitative data analysis of career aspirations – Mean	
Particulars	**Findings**
Career Aspirations	Majority of the data (52.4%) join profession but no proper guidance (18%)- did not have any clarity about professional fields (12.7%)- want to adopt their hobbies as their career (7.6%)- Government Jobs (3.9%)- Aviation and Hotel management (3.03%)- Not allowed for higher education (1.5%)- aspire for higher education abroad (0.9%)- Entrepreneurs
Guidance to choose a profession	Majority of the girls (70.14%) had their career aspirations to join profession such as Teachers, Chartered Accountant, but they didnot have any guidance to choose a profession, and also majority of them were not having any idea about different professional field as well.
Family permission for higher studies	43.9% said Yes 21%- said No 29.1- said Not sure

Implications	From the data derived for the career aspirations, it can be said that majority of the girls aspired to join professional after completing their higher studies, but they did not have any guidance about various professional fields.
	Moreover, majority of the girls were not permitted for higher studies or were not sure of whether they will be permitted for the same.
	Hence, human development theory in this context, it can be said that there is lack of opportunities provided to excel by the associated stakeholders.
Suggestions:	The schools can play a role of facilitator to bridge the gap between the lack of information and the students as the beneficiaries, which shall be an investment for the future resources of the country.

(Section-D)- Findings related to the Indirect Impact of community and government towards the education of Muslim girls: This section of the study indicates the indirect impact of community and the government on the education of Muslim girls; such as the financial and non-financial support of the community towards the higher education of girls, the awareness about the government scholarships and schemes among the beneficiaries.

Table:5.3.0 Community and government support as an indirect impact over the educational status of Muslim girls

Qualitative data analysis on educational status among Muslims- ContentAnalysis		
Community Support for Higher education	Views from Teachers 48.35% lack of Family support (Community pressure) 46.15% Social and Religious obligations 5.5% Financial scarcity	Views from Parents 55%- Advised by community for not permitting daughters for Higher Education. 45%- The rate has increased
Findings	It can be interpreted that from the response of teachers and parents that because of conservative mindset of the community and lower educational status among parents, there is less preference given over the higher education for girls and under the influence of the community, the parents or the family members do not provide financial/ motivational support to the girls to pursue higher education.	
Support by NGO/VO	Views from Teachers 54.94% had awareness 28.57% No such aid given 5.49% support from rural communities	Views from Parents 76%- are not aware 19%- aware and availing benefit 5%- aware but not availing
Findings	It can be interpreted that there is lack of awareness about the NGO/VO offering the services to facilitate the educational progress for girls among the beneficiaries i.e (the parents),	
Government Support for Higher education	From Teachers 83.15% were about government schemes	From Parents 13% were aware and only 8% are scheme beneficiaries

Findings	Majority of the teachers were aware about pre-metric and post- metric scholarships, as the scholarships have to be managed by the school itself, though the data shows lack of awareness about the scheme.
Implications	There are efforts by the government to regulate and facilitates the education especially for the minorities, but there is lack of awareness among the masses
Suggestions	Awareness aspect is a major lacking aspect, and this can be taken up by the school authorities and teachers as an educational stakeholder, they should take proactive steps pertaining to spreading awareness related to the beneficiaries' schemes as well as on the importance of education. It is with these efforts only "Return on Investment" shall be evident

5.4 Major Findings: This Section of the chapter describes the major findings of the study as:

A. Findings related to background study information

B. Findings related to elementary study information

C. Findings related to direct impact of the study

D. Findings related to indirect impact of the study

5.4.1 Section-A) Findings related to the study background:

School Profile: Majority of the Muslim Managed schools chosen for the study were private schools who had their inception during 1980's, was offering Gujarati language as a medium of instruction and its association with Gujarat Secondary and Higher Secondary Education board. Widely, the schools were co-education school and were offering the commerce stream in higher secondary classes. The schools possessed more female teachers.

Profile of Principals and Higher Secondary school teachers: majority of the schools had male principals, having B.Ed. as their educational qualification and possessed good academic experience of more than 10 years, whereas majority of the schools had more of female teachers in their higher secondary classes with B.Ed. as their educational qualification and work experience of more than 10 years.

Profile of the Muslim girls: Majority of the girls belonged to nuclear families possessing the monthly income of less than 10,000 ₹

Profile of the Parents of Muslim girls: Majority of parents were in the age group of 31-40 years, majority of fathers were educated till secondary classes, whereas majority of the mothers were educated till primary classes. Looking in to the occupation, majority of the fathers were either having small scale business, and number of girls whose fathers were daily wage earners were also more. Comparatively, the majority of mothers were home makers. The families that fall within the income level of 10,001-20,000 ₹ were also more.

The findings shows that there was lack of higher education among both the parents of the Muslim girls. Further, comparison indicates that the education level among mothers is lower than the fathers. The occupation status also indicates that majority of the parents were managing their own business or were daily wage earners whereas mothers were the homemakers. Therefore, it can be said that because of the lower educational status among the parents, there is less participation of parents towards the workforce and further comparing the participation of male and females, females are more home makers.

5.4.2 Section-B) - Findings related to the elementary information of the study: Objective: 1 a) To study the number of Muslim girls in secondary and higher secondary classes in and around Vadodara.

About the Enrolment of Muslim Girls in Schools: Majority of the enrolment of Muslim girls were found in private schools. The class strength of Muslim girls in secondary classes was 50-100, and it reduced to less than 50 in higher secondary classes. This shows that the drop-out rates of Muslim girls are higher in higher secondary classes.

Objective: 2 a) Exploring the role of school as an educational stakeholder Infrastructural facility in schools: Majority of the private schools were having inadequate facilities of library, computer lab/ science lab, inadequate classroom facilities, improper hygiene and sanitation facilities. Whereas government and aided schools were in a better position in provision of such facilities. Additionally, Government and aided schools were also providing other facilities such as prayer room and washing area for the afternoon prayers within the school premises.

Impact of Infrastructural facilities on School Enrolment: 76.19% of Principals and 79.12% of Teachers said that availability of good infrastructural facilities in school is a decision-making factor for parents as well as girls studying to get themselves enrolled in good schools with adequate infrastructural facilities.

Future plan of Principals on Infrastructural Development: 12.08%- Focused on Technological

Upgradation, 7.69%- Focused on Infrastructural development, 3.29%- They do not have autonomy and power to take decisions 76.94%- Not responded.

Teacher's views on class performance of Muslim girls: 41.75%- Academic performance is good, 25.27%- Need encouragement/ motivation.

Teacher's views on reasons of lower enrolment of Muslim girls in higher education: 62.63%- Lack of family support/ a smaller number of universities for girls and 41.75%- Less priority of girl's education/ conservative mindset of the community. Hence because of the lack of family support and a smaller number of universities only for girls, girls are not allowed for higher education.

5.4.3 Section-C)- Findings related to the Direct Impact of Schools towards the education of Muslim girls:

Objective: 2 a) Exploring the role of school as an educational stakeholder

Training of Teachers: The schools lack in organizing a need-based training programme, the training programmes are organized once a year by the school management in all the type of school- private, Government and aided.

Impact of Teacher's Counselling on retention of Muslim girls higher secondary classes: 70.32% yes it helps in retention (Through Counselling to parents/ girls and sometimes home visits), 23.07%- Partially was able to retain (Through Counselling to parents/ girls and sometimes home visits), 6.59%- No they were not successful. Hence it can be said that the teachers are really making efforts to retain the girls in school by adopting various measures as a part of their ethical responsibility, however the investment done is not giving the expected outcome.

Views of girls on subjective knowledge among teachers: 38.78%- Private schools, 24.54%- Government schools, and 16.66%- aided schools, hence majority 79.98% of girls were satisfied with the subjective knowledge of their teachers.

Use of Innovative Pedagogies by teachers in classroom teaching: majority of the teachersare using textbooks and supplement the classroom teaching by some examples.

Initiatives taken for student's academic development: 38.09% of schools are organizingelocution, essay writing, science exhibition, for the development of cognitive, innovative, leadership qualities among the students by planning and organizing such activities, subsequently encouraging active participation for further enhancement of skills.

Initiatives taken for students' social development: 28.57%- Conducting Expert's session, counselling by teachers (Govt, private and aided), hence, there are initiatives planned and undertaken for the development of the students by the school authorities as well as teachers are also performing the roles of the facilitator by taking counselling session so as to retain the students in higher secondary classes as well as motivating them for higher studies.

5.4.4 (Section-C)- Findings related to the Direct Impact of Schools towards the educationof Muslim girls

Objective: 2 b) Exploring the role of parents of Muslim girls as an educationalstakeholder

Parental satisfaction with the availability of infrastructural facilities in school: Negative correlation was observed between the parents as an influencer and other related aspects with the school. They are not concerned about the infrastructural facilities, neither are demanding.

Reason of Enrolment of daughters in Muslim managed schools: 46%- A school with good infrastructural facilities and Muslim culture, 41%- A Muslim cultured school, nearby residence and a low budget school. Hence it can be said that parents give less preference towards the availability of good infrastructural facilities in school and the quality education, but rather prefer to send their daughters in schools which is nearby their residential areas and the schools which has Muslim culture in terms of their Uniforms, allowed to do prayer on time.

Parents views on teaching quality in schools: Majority of the parents 62% were satisfied with the quality in education rendered by teachers in schools.

Parents views on guidance provided by teachers to students: 49% of parents said that theschools' teachers are providing guidance for higher education as well as for performance improvement to both the parents as well to their parents, especially when they come to schools during the result timings.

Parents views on impact of schooling on Social and Psychological development of students: 54% of parents shared optimistic development of their wards due to their schooling.

Parents occupation and their support for higher education: Majority of the fathers who were in service sector (n=15) realized the importance of education and said that they will support their daughter's education.

Parents views on girls' safety in schools: 53% of parents said that education and is taken care of by the school management.

Acceptance of parent's suggestion: 57% of parents said that the Parent Teacher's Meetings (PTM) are organized and the suggestions shared by the parents during meetings is well taken into consideration and are implemented as well.

Parents views on lower higher educational status among Muslim girls: Majority of the parents 43%, said that the Muslim girls are not sent for higher education, and considers financial constraints and parental restrictions as the main reasons for hindering the higher educational status among Muslim.

Parents views on supporting their daughters in attaining higher education: 31%- (Mothers) and 24% (Fathers) for their own better future, 9%- (Mothers) and 11% of (Fathers) Respectable position in the community and 7% (Mothers) and 3% of (Fathers) not allowed to go for higher studies. Hence Majority of the mothers are willing to support the higher education of their daughters.

5.4.5 Objective 3: To study the home environment of Muslim girls

Type of Family and Monthly Income: Muslim girls came from a nuclear family background, with majority of them having monthly income to be less than 10,000 ₹ per month.

Monthly Income and enrollment in schools: Majority of girls have their family monthly income less than 10,000 ₹, yet they are enrolled with private Muslim managed schools.

Parents views on Guidance, Monitoring and Academic Help to their daughters: Majority of the mothers are having their education till primary classes, and hence they are not able to help in academics of their children, however, they monitor related aspects such as punctuality, they instruct their wards for the regularity and punctuality, to focus on studies when their wards at home and constant reminders about their homework.

Participation of Parents in Parent Teachers Meetings: Because of lack of education, there is less preference given towards the education of girls and hence parental involvement is found to be less among the parents of the Muslim girls.

Autonomy to girls in going to school/coaching classes: Majority of the girls are allowed to go independently to school / coaching classes.

Responsibility of Domestic chores/ Compulsions/ freedom to take decisions: There is no autonomy/ freedom given to girls in terms of taking decision pertaining to the educational as well as recreational needs, they have compulsions in terms of their attire.

5.4.6 (Section-C)- Findings related to the Direct Impact of Schools towards the education of Muslim girls

Objective 4: To find out the career aspirations of Muslim girls.

Career Aspirations and Guidance to choose a profession: Majority of the girls (70.14%) had their career aspirations to join profession such as Teachers, Chartered Accountant, but they did not have any guidance to choose a profession, nor any clarity about various professional fields.

Family permission for higher studies: 43.9% said Yes, 21%- said No, 29.1-said Not sure.Hence it can be said that majority of the girls were not permitted for higher studies or were not sure of whether they will be permitted to go for higher studies.

5.4.7 (Section-D)- Findings related to the Indirect Impact of community andgovernment towards the education of Muslim girls.

Objective 2 c) Exploring the role of community as an Educational Stakeholder

Community Support for Higher education: 48.35% of teachers and 55% of parents said that conservative mindset of the community, lower educational status among parents, thereis less preference towards the higher education for girls, Community pressure for not sendingthe daughters is also one reason why parents/ family members do not provide financial/ motivational support to the girls to pursue higher education.

Educational Support by NGO/VO: 54.94% of teachers had awareness about the educational support provided by NGO/VO's, whereas, 76% of parents were not aware. Hence it can be said that there is lack of awareness about the NGO/VO's offering the services to facilitate the educational progress for girls among the beneficiaries i.e (the parents).

Objective 2 d) Exploring the role of government as an Educational Stakeholder

Government Support for Higher education: 83.15% of Teachers were aware about governmentschemes and 13% of parents were having awareness about various government schemes and programmes and only 8% of them were availing its benefits.

5.5 Discussions of Results:

From the findings of the study, it can be said that the enrolment of Muslim girls in school have increased over a period of time, however the study shows high dropout rate of Muslim girls from secondary and higher secondary classes. Thus, this indicates that still, the ratio of girls moving from secondary to higher secondary has not given the satisfactory results. Tremendous persistent efforts and measures are required as education is the only medium to bring positive social as well as economic changes within the society.

Identifying the reasons for the lower higher educational status, the study finds various socio-economic factors, **((Siddiqui 1987); (Mondal 1997); (Begum 1999); (Chaturvedi 2004); (Hasan and Menon 2005); (Pande 2006))** one of which is conservative mindset among the community, which is due to lower education among previous generation (Parents/ other family members). The other factors include weaker socio-economic status, which is also a subsequently of lower representation among Muslim community skilled workforce of the nation.

Another associated is less preference given towards the higher education of girls, because of various socio- cultural beliefs prevailing among Muslim Community ((**Waseem 2012**); **(Hussain 2018); (Saha 2020))** which deprives Muslim women from attaining higher education, consequently restricting women's ability as decision makers in the family.)

Identifying the role and contribution of associated stakeholders, majority of the researches undertaken focused on the reasons, the dropout rates of the girls from the schools, Hence, it can be said that along with identifying the reasons for the lower higher educational status among Muslim girls, the role of all the associated stakeholders such as schools, Teachers, the parents, the community, the government comprehensively, need to be focused on , as the stakeholders' initiatives and contributions make a huge impact in bringing about social as well as economic change in the economy of the nation.

5.6 Conclusions of the Study:

Pertaining to the availability of Infrastructural facilities in school: The private schools have all the authorities and have the autonomy in taking decisions pertaining to the upgradation of basic as well as educational infrastructural facilities within the school premises, yet the schools covered under the study are lacking in providing such basic educational as well as infrastructural facilities in schools.

Pertaining to Higher Educational Status among Muslim Girls: There is high drop-out rate of Muslim girls in standard XI and XII, because of lack of education, lack of awareness, financial crunches within the family, there is lack of sensitization towards education, the outcome of which is less enrolment of girls in higher education, which subsequently impacts their contribution in the social development as well as the economic contribution of the nation.

Pertaining to the Training of Teachers: Training comprise an essential part in an educational institution. The ANOVA Single factor test conducted for the study also reveals that the teachers training, pedagogy used and implemented, and availability of infrastructural facilities have a strong impact on the student's development.

Pertaining to Student's development: The investment done by the schools by organizing remedial classes, counselling by teachers, various activities and competitions organized by the schools is not giving expected returns on the investment done.

Pertaining to Home environment of Muslim girls: Because of lack of education among the parents, and lower family income among the families and due to safety issues, they are enrolling their daughters which are nearby the residential areas. Lack of education among parents also prevents them to get involved in the education of their children.

Along with the social and economic factors, they are also very much under cultural influence, which restricts their mobility, which subsequently is impacting on their decision of having professional careers.

Pertaining to Career Aspirations: The restrictions, lack of awareness and societal pressure are responsible for lack of opportunities provided to excel by the associated stakeholders.

5.7 Suggestions from the Study:

Suggestions for the School as an Internal Stakeholder:

1. To bring in the new culture of education and confirming sustainability.

Training: Comprehensive training of the teaching staff is to be planned and organized on a frequent basis which should cater to the concept of school management comprising of use of innovative pedagogies, ensuring quality education, with the intention of developing creative, innovative thinking abilities among the students, which subsequently will developinterest in the student population for the higher education.

Infrastructural development: For the usage of innovative techniques and pedagogies, an "Investment" to upgrade the human resources is to be done especially for the needed infrastructural development such as availability and access to computer labs, library, audio- visual devices within the classrooms, certain basic hygienic and potable drinking water facilities in the schools. Additionally, the schools should make their investment in overall development by encouraging students to participate in co-curricular activities also leading to physical, socio- emotional development as well.

Guidance and Counselling to the students: It was observed from the data, that students lackbasic ideas on availability of various career guidance, so an "investment" by conducting seminars and workshops on career guidance can be given to the students, which shall bring its return on investment among the future generation.

Guidance and Counselling to parents: The schools should also frequently organize the seminars, workshops, the talks for the parents of the girls which gives them importance of education, the available financial assistance for girl's education by the government as well as non-government organizations, which will in the long run increase the educational status of Muslim girls. The educational upliftment from one set of society will definitely bring in improvement in the other segments of the society. Teachers can play a vital role in disseminating the authentic information for the students and ensuring the developmental pace of the girls.

Record Keeping for the Sustainable development of girls: The Schools should adopt a measure of maintaining the track record of girls who join in higher education after completing standard XII, which will further motivate the upcoming generation for higher education.

Suggestions for the parents as an External Stakeholder

Enabling safe learning environment and motivating girls at home.

Through Involvement: Increase in participation of parents in students learning, showing involvement in terms of taking regular feedbacks and updates about the daughter's progress from the teachers will strengthen the ground of monitoring of parents and will also serve asa motivational factor among the girls. The third stage of Maslow's theory of hierarchy of needs of love and belonging can be linked herewith, as the love, care, interest from the parentswill pave its way for girls moving for the fourth stage of achieving self-esteem and recognition, ultimately, they shall begin developing the interest for higher education throughsupport and motivation from parents as the findings of the study suggests that the decision of parents is very detrimental in decision making for girls.

Suggestions For Community as an External Stakeholder

Creating Psychological safety and empathetic understanding: Performing the role of supporter: The study data reveals that the Muslim community is in the contemporary situation is performing the role an obstructor rather than the supporter. Hence the role reversal of the community is required in following ways:

a. Collaboration of various stakeholders of the community such as schools, the educationist, the social workers, the members from NGO/VO's should work on the modus operandi of sensitizing the community on the matters connected with the higher education of girls through organizing frequent seminars, expert lectures, talks at various occasions.

b. Correct leaders need to be identified from the community, there is a strong need to identify the accurate, educated and neutral leadership from the community member, who have influencing potentials towards the other masses of the community, so that they can spread right information among the masses.

Identification and collaboration with the social workers/ the professionals need to be developed with an intention to develop a healthy collaboration among the school management, teaching staff, the parents of the girls, in order to have a wholistic learning and further advancement of the community and the nations as a whole.

Adopting the Successful Models from the community: The successful models of the schools which are established at various places by eminent and the influential community leaders in the rural areas of the city such as Kalla school at Karjan, Hanifa school at Borsad, Refai school at kalol shall be adopted to increase the level of higher education in the urban areas also.

Suggestions for the Government as an External Stakeholder

1) Leveraging the best practices within the school network and undergoing partnership/collaboration with grass root level organization: The government should perform the role of regulator by analyzing the best possible practices adopted by the schools, should include them as a part of the school management, and should make a "learning model"

for the schools which can be utilized in the interest and benefits of the students as well as the teaching staff, within the framework of New Education Policy 2020

The government should also look in to certain revision in terms of teacher's appointments, the compensation paid to the teachers in the policies as it is the primary motivational factor for any individual to work with dedication and commitment and perform to the best of one's capacity

5.8 Summary table of the Suggestions

	Suggestions
For Schools	Should develop People centric approach- and "investment" to be done for providing infrastructural facilities, especially the Private schools who have the autonomy in their budgeting
	Need based training programmes for teachers – covering "Schoolmanagement"- Planning, Organizing, Directing, and Controlling
	Career guidance and Counselling sessions to students, personality development, interpersonal skills should be organized
	Counselling and awareness sessions for the parents can be organized by the schools to motivate and counsel parents to send their daughters for higher education
	Awareness on various financial and non-financial aid should be given to parents and the students to avail the maximum benefit of the same.
	Seminars, lectures, talks – importance of education should be organized for parents

	Follow up of the girls going for higher education after HSC should be done –model for the other students from the schools.
For Community	Stakeholders from the community- should spread awareness on the importance of education
	NGO/ VO's- Should approach the schools and provide information to students
For Government	Effective check on the implementation of the schemes and programmes.

Figure:5.9 Theoretical Framework Based on the Study Findings

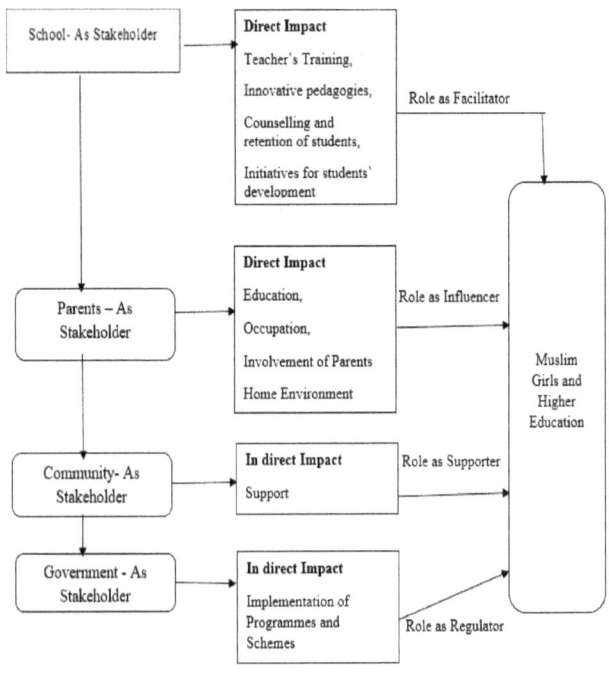

5.9 Explanation of the Theoretical Frame Work

From the above diagrammatic theoretical framework, following are the roles of various stakeholders associated with the education of Muslim girls in and around city of Vadodara,

Role of School: The Schools performs the role of Facilitator towards the education of Muslim girl. Various components like need based training to teachers, innovative pedagogies incorporated by the teachers in their classroom teaching, retention of Muslim girls in higher secondary classes through teachers counselling, and the initiatives and activities planned and undertaken by the school for the Physical, Cognitive and Social development of Muslim girls, have direct impact towards the higher education of Muslim girls.

Role of Parents: Another important stakeholder identified by the current study are the parents of the Muslim girls, The associated aspects like the parental education, the occupation, their involvement towards the education of their daughters and the home environment have direct impact and they perform the role of an influencer towards the higher education of Muslim girls.

Role of Community: Community is also identified as one key stakeholder towards the higher education of Muslim girls. The support, the beliefs, practices, value of higher education has in direct impact towards the higher education of girls, as it varies upon person to person, family to family, region to region. The support rendered by the community plays an important role as that of a supporter towards the higher education of Muslim girls.

Role of Government: Regulation is very much essential for effective management of any institutions. Education as an institution needs government as a regulatory mechanism by levying and implementing various programmes, schemes to support the higher education of Muslim girls, which performs the role of a regulator.

5.10 SCOPE OF FURTHER RESEARCH

- The Present study covered Muslim managed schools offering higher secondary classes. Theseschools noted to have wide variation in terms of availability of infrastructural facilities, aspects related to teachers such as training, innovative pedagogies depending upon the type of school. Further Management research on education Management of girls (comprising of all the communities) can be undertaken in other schools of Baroda city.

- Need Assessment can be undertaken to identify the gaps in the available infrastructural facilities for girls in various schools.

- Further research in Higher education institutes can also be undertaken to know their motivation and career aspiration of Muslim girls.

- A study on contribution of Muslim girls/ women's – who have been successful in achieving their career aspirations to education of girls can be undertaken.

- An Impact assessment of various initiatives undertaken by various NGO's/ VO's towards the education of Muslim girls can be undertaken as a research study.

Need assessment of all the Muslim managed schools and educational institutions, can be undertaken.

References

Books

A

Aggarwal J.C (2005), Reprint edition," Basic Ideas in Education", *Shipra Publications.*

Delhi, ISBN:81-7541-086-8.

Aggarwal J.C and Gupta S (2007) "Curriculum Development 2005 – Towards Learning without burden and quality of Education- An Evaluation", *Shipra Publications* Delhi, ISBN: 978-81-7541-263-7.

B

Babalola J. (2003) "Budget Preparation and Expenditure Control in Education. *"In*

Babalola J.B. (ed.) Basic Text in Educational Planning. *Ibadan. Awemark Printers*

Bagin D and Donald R (2001) (2005), The school and community relation, 7th and 11th edition, London Alyan and Bacon.

Balsara M (2006) "Principles of Curriculum Reconstruction", *Kanishka publishers, Distributors, New Delhi.*

Begum (1998), "Education and Muslim, Women in Rural West Bengal in *M.A.Siddiqui (ed), Muslims in Free India: Their Social Profile and Problems*', New Delhi: Institute of Objective Studies, 1998

Begum (1999). "Indian Muslim", in Education and the Muslim Women, ed. *by Noor Mohammad, 154-172.* Jaypur and New Delhi: Rawat Publication.

Benn, T. (2002). Muslim women in teacher training: issues of gender, 'race' and religion, in: *London, Routledge.*

Brock C and Cammish N (1997), "Factors affecting female participation in education in seven developing countries". *Second edition, Department of International development, London.* ISBN: 1861920 -65- 2

C

Chaturvedi (2003), "Encyclopedia of Muslim Women*", New Delhi, Commonwealth*

E

Engineer (2002), "Islam in India: The Impact of Civilizations", *Shipra Publications.*

ISBN 81-7541-115-5.

F

Fagerlind, A. & Saha, L.J. (1997). Education and national developments", *ReedEducational and Professional Publishers Ltd.* New Delhi

Freeman, R.E. (1984)," Strategic management: A stakeholder approach", *Boston: Pitman*

Fuller, B. & Liang, X. (1999). Which girls stay in school? The influence of family economy, social demands, and ethnicity in South Africa.: *National Academy Press,* Washington, DC

G

Govinda, R & Diwan, R. (1998), "Community Participation and Empowerment in PrimaryEducation", *SAGE Publication,* New Delhi.

H

Hasan Z, Menon R (2004), "Unequal Citizens: A Study of Muslim Women in India",

Oxford University Press, New Delhi

J

Jain S (1988), "The Process of modernization in India and the status of Muslim Women",Status of women, *Print well publishers, Jaipur*

K

Kalra V (2008) "School Efficiency", *APH Publishing Corporation, New Delhi. ISBN:978-81- 313-0207-1.*

Kapur R (2018), "Factors Influencing the Student's Academic Performance iin SecondarySchools in India". *University of Delhi, India*

Kazi (1999), "Muslim Women in India, *Minority Rights Group International, London*

M

Menon (1981), "Status of Muslim Women in India- A Case Study of Kerala", *Uppal Publications, New Delhi,*

Mondal (1997), "Educational Status of Muslim: Problems, Prospects and Priorities", *Inter India Publications, New Delhi*

P

Predoomed, V.F (1991), "Educational administration, applied concepts and theoretical perspectives for students and practitioners", *Lagos: JOJA Educational Research and Publishers Limited* Publishing Inc.

R

Richards and Thomas S.C Farell (2005), "Professional development for language teachers: strategies for teacher learning", *Cambridge University Press,* ISBN: 13 978 0 521 84911 1.

S

Siddiqui (1987), " Muslim Woman in transition: A Social Profile, *Harnam Publications, New Delhi*

Conference /Research Papers/ Dissertations

Abdullah M.Q (2017), "The Relationship between Social Skills, Self-Esteem and Big FivePersonality Factors among Children", *Psychology and Psychological research International Journal*, Vol-2, Issue-3, Medwin publishers, retrieved from https://medwinpublishers.com/PPEamonRIJ/PPRIJ16000129.pdf on 27/11/2020.

Abdullah (2020), Educational Status of Muslims in India: An Overview / Scope for Improvement, retrieved from

https://muslimmirror.com/eng/educational-status-of-muslims-in-india-an-overview-scope-for-improvement/

Abena, F. D. (1991). The Emancipation of Women an African Perspective. Accra: *Ghana Universities Press.* ww.jstor.org/stable/525186 accessed from https://amity.edu/UserFiles/aibs/a94f2019%20AIJJS_72-84.pdf on 28/12/2020

Ahmed J (2016), "Problems and Prospects of Muslim women's Education: A sociological study of poonch district of Jammu and Kashmir", Ph.D. thesis submitted to Department of Sociology, Aligarh Muslim University. https://shodhganga.inflibnet.ac.in/handle/10603/152465 on 30/12/2020

Akhtar, S, (1996), "Do Girls Have a Higher School Drop-out Rate than Boys? A Hazard Rate Analysis of Evidence from a Third World City". Urban Studies,33(1): 49-62.

Akujieze, M.O. (2003), "Influence of Socio-Economic Background on Achievement in Mathematics at the Senior Secondary School Level in Ibadan North Local Government Area of Oyo State", Un published M.Ed. Project: University of Ibadan

Alavi, H. R. (2008), "Nearness to god: A perspective on Islamic education. Religious Education", 103(1), 5-21. Retrieved from http://doi: 10.1080/00344080701807361on 12/04/2019.

Alison A (1997), "Leadership and Community Participation: Four Case studies", ERIC, ISSN:0882-1832.

Almendarez L,(2010) "Human Capital Theory: Implications for Educational Development"- Belize country conference, Nov-21 -24-2001/ 2010, university of west indies retrieved from
http://cavehill.uwi.edu/bnccde/belize/conference/papers/filename.htm/l on 3/11/2020

Alvarez (2008), "The Relationship of Teacher Quality and Student, Achievement in Elementary Schools from the New York City", Dissertation submitted Faculty of the college of education, TUI University.

Andargie Washiun Abi (2013), "Status of Community Participation in The Management of Government Secondary Schools of Agnwa Zone at Gambella Regional State", un-published master's thesis, Jimmy University, Institute of Education and Professional Development Studies, department Of Educational Planning and Management

Anderson, E, & Trivette, P. (1995). The effects of four components of parental involvement on eighth grade student achievement: structural analysis of NELS-88 data. School Psychology Review, 24(2), 299-318, retrieved from https://eric.ed.gov/?id=EJ587377 on 29/11/2020

Annu S and Mishra S (2013), "Impact of Extra- Curricular activities on students in private schools of Lucknow district, International Journal of Humanities and Social Science Invention. ISSN (Online): 2319 – 7722, ISSN(Print):2319-7714, retrieved from\https://www.researchgate.net/publication/257536354_Impact_of_extra curricular_activities_on_students_in_private_school_of_Lucknow_District on 1/1/2021.

Argyris, C. (1958), "Some problems in conceptualizing organizational climate: A casestudy of a bank", Administrative Science Quarterly, Vol. 2, pp.501-520.

Ashraf, S. A. (1985), "New Horizons in Muslim Education", Cambridge: The IslamicAcademy.

Asia Baka (2010), "The Need for Effective Facility Management in Schools in Nigeria", New York Science journal, ISSN: 1554-0200, retrieved from http://www.sciencepub.net/newyork/0102/02_0366_Asiabaka_FACILITIES. pdf on21/11/2020.

Asif, M., & Khan, M. M. (2010), "Comparative Study of Analytical and Synthetic Methodsof Teaching Mathematics", *Journal of International Academic Research*, Vol-10, Issue-7.

Atayi, J. B. (2008). Disabling Barriers to Girls' Primary Education in Aura District (Uganda) – An Intersectional Analysis. A Research Paper presented impartial fulfillmentof the requirements for obtaining the degree of Masters of Arts in Development studies.

Athman, J and M. Manroe, (2004), "The effects of environment-based education on students' achievement motivation, *The Journal of Interpretation Research*, 9(1), pp. 9– 25

B

Baluyos (2019) studied, "Teachers' Job Satisfaction and Work Performance", Scientific Research, accessed from https://www.scirp.org/journal/paperinformation.aspx?paperid=94433

Bano F (2017), "Educational Status of Muslim Women in India: An Overview", IOSR, Journal of Humanities and Social Sciences, Vol- 22.

Baradei L and Amin K (2010), "Community Participation in Education: A case study of the board of trustees experience in Fayoum governate in Egypt", African Education Review7 (1) retrieved from

https://www.researchgate.net/publication/233082182_Community_participation_in_education_A

_case_study_of_the_Boards_of_Trustees'_experience_in_the_Fayoum_gove norate_in_Egypt on 6/12/2020.

Barbhuyan (2017) studied, "Problems and Prospects of Muslim women in HigherEducation, Ph.D. thesis submitted to Faculty of Arts, Gulati University.

https://shodhganga.inflibnet.ac.in/handle/10603/224382?mode=full on30/12/2020

Basumatry R, (2012), "School Dropout across Indian States and UTs: An EconometricStudy, International Research Journal of Social Sciences, Vol-1 (4), ISSN:2319–3565, taken fromhttp://www.isca.in/IJSS/Archive/v1/i4/5.ISCA-IRJSS-2012-061.pdf

on4/12/2020.

Bhalotra & Heady (2004); Basu, Das and Dutta, (2003) on, "Child Farm Labour: TheWealth Paradox", the world economic Bank review, DOI: 10.1093/wber/lhg017.

Bhat D, Khurshid F, and Hussain N (2011), Islam, gender and Education; a case study ofJammu and Kashmir, *Asia pacific journal of social sciences,* vol-3,2, ISSN: 0975-5942 Bhatnagar and Sharma (1992), "A Study of the Relationship Between Parental Education

and Academic achievement in a Semi- Rural Setting", Psychological Studies, 37, 2,126-129.

Biswas and Mukhopadyaya (2018), , "Marital Status and Women Empowerment in India", from https://medcraveonline.com/SIJ/marital-status-and-women-empowerment- in-india.html on 7/1/2021.

Boruah (2017), "A Study on availability of Educational Facilities for the Teachers and thestudents, *IJEDR* | Volume 5, Issue 4 | ISSN: 2321-9939, from https://www.ijedr.org/papers/IJEDR1704156.pdf on 7/1/2021.

Breen, R., and Goldthorpe, J. H (1997), "Explaining Educational Differentials: Towards a Formal Rational Action Theory", Rationality and Society, 9 (3): 275–305

Brookfield M (2013), undertook a study on "The Impacts of Education: A Case Study ofMuslim Women in Ngaoundéré, Cameroon, accessed from SIT digital collection from https://digitalcollections.sit.edu/cgi/viewcontent.cgi?referer= https://www.goo gle.co.in/&httpsredir=1&article=2746&context=isp_collectio n on 6/1/2021

Brown P and Park A (2002), "Education and Poverty In Rural China, Economics of EducationReview,Vol-21,Issue-6.Retrieved from https://www.sciencedirect.com/science/article/abs/pii/S02727 75701000401 on 4/12/2020

Bruns, Barbara; Deon Filmer and Harry Anthony Patrinos (2011), "Making Schools Work: New Evidence on Accountability Reforms" cited by Pradhan M (2011), "Improving Educational Quality through Enhancing Community Participation: Results from a Randomized Field Experiment in Indonesia".

Buckley, J., Schneider, M., & Shang, Y. (2004b). Fix it and They Might Stay: School Facility Quality and Teacher Retention in Washington, DC. Teachers College Record, 107, 1107-1123. on, March 1,2019

C

Carroll, B., & Hollinshead, G. (1993). Ethnicity and Conflict in Physical Education, British Educational Research Journal, 19(1), 59-75.

Chandra R and Azimuddin S (2013), studied "Influence of Socio-Economic Status on Academic Achievement of Secondary School Students of Lucknow City, *International Journal of Scientific and Engineering Research-* Vol-4, issue11, retrieved from
https://www.researchgate.net/publication/259322012_Influen ce_of_Socio_Economic_S
tatus_on_Academic_achievement_of_lucknow_city on 1/1/2021.

Chaudhari N and Nagwanshee R (2019) "A comparative study between Rural and UrbanSchools with special reference to Infrastructural facilities", Research Review, *International journal of Multi-disciplinary*, vol-4 ,(6) accessed from
https://www.academia.edu/39606028/A_Comparative_Study _between_Rural_and_

urban_Schools_with_special_reference_to_Infrastructure_Facilities_in

_the_Anuppur_District_of_Madhya_Pradesh on 30/12/2020

Chauhan V, (2016), "Conceptualizing Education in Human Development paradigm", *International Journal of Humanities and Social Science studies* (IJHSSS), Volume-III, Issue-II, ISSN: 2349-6959 (Online), ISSN: 2349-6711 (Print)

Chege, F., & Sifuna, D.N. (2006). Girls' and Women's education in Kenya gender perspectives and trends, www.library.unescoiicba.org/.../Girls%20Education/.../Girls%20and%2

Chhaya M (1998), "Effective Schools", A paper from "Contemporary Thoughts on Education", - Commemorative Volume, Society for Educational Research and Development, Baroda.

D

Dalziel D and Henthorne K, TNS Social research on "Parent's / carer'sattitudes Towards School Attendance", *Taylor Nelson Sofres*, ISBN 1 84478416 9, retrieved from https://dera.ioe.ac.uk/5548/1/RR618.pdf on 29/11/2020 Devi L (2014), "Socio- Economic development of Muslim Women: Impact of Education", *Indian Journal of Public Administration*, 07, Vol, 60, (3), doi,10.1177/0019556120140323

E

Evangelista de Carvalho Filho, (2008); "Household income as a determinant of child labourand school enrolment in Brazil "working paper IMF WP08/241Faisal, (2014) "Influenceof Parent Socio- Economic Status on their Involvement at Home",

International Journal of Humanities and Social Sciences, Vol-5,NO-4,retrieved from\https://www.researchgate.net/publication/306090710_The_Influence_of_Parental_Socioeconomic_Status_on_Their_Involvement_at_Home on 28/11/2020

F

Fauzia (2017), "Right to education: status of Muslim girl children in rural Uttar Pradesh", *International journal of development research,* vol-7, ISSN:2230-9926, http://doi.org/10.37118

Faisal. (2014), The Influence of Parental Socioeconomic Status on Their Involvement at Home", *International Journal of Humanities and Social Science.* vol. 5. 146-154.

Firdaus B (2017), "Educational Status of Muslim Women in India: An overview", *IOSR, journal of humanities and social sciences,* vol-22, Issue-6, e-ISSN: 2279-0837, p-ISSN:2279-0845.

Fredrikson (2004), "Quality Education: The Teacher's Key Role", working paper, retrieved fromhttps://www.basicknowledge101.com/pdf/literacy/Quality%20Education%20 and%20the %20Key%20Role%20of%20Teachers.pdf on 15/04/2019

G

Galloway S (2014) "The Impact of Islam as a Religion and Muslim women on Gender Equality: A Phenomenological Research Study", Ph.D. dissertation submitted to Graduate school of Humanities and Social Sciences, of Nova South Eastern University accessed from https://nsuworks.nova.edu/cgi/viewcontent.cgi?article=1013&context=shssdcaretdon 30/12/2020

Gillies D, (2015), "Human Capital Theory in Education", Encyclopedia of EducationalPhilosophy and Theory", *Springer Science, Business Media* Singapore,

Glick, P. & Sahn, D.E. (2000). Schooling of girls and boys in a West African country:the effects of parental education, income, and household structure. Economics of Education Review, 19, 63–87.

Gorham & Diane M. Millette (1997), "A comparative analysis of teacher and student perceptions of sources of motivation and demotivation in college classes", Communication Education,46:4,245-261, DOI:10.1080/03634529709379099

Gouda et, al (2013), "Government Verses Private Schools in India, An assessment ofphysical infrastructure, schooling cost and performance", *International journal of Sociology and social policy,* Vol-33,No-11,accessedfrom

International Journal of Humanities and Social Sciences, Vol-5,NO-4,retrieved from\https://www.researchgate.net/publication/306090710_The_Influence_of_Parental_Socioeconomic_Status_on_Their_Involvement_at_Home on 28/11/2020

F

Fauzia (2017), "Right to education: status of Muslim girl children in rural Uttar Pradesh", *International journal of development research,* vol-7, ISSN:2230-9926, http://doi.org/10.37118

Faisal. (2014), The Influence of Parental Socioeconomic Status on Their Involvement at Home", *International Journal of Humanities and Social Science.* vol. 5. 146-154.

Firdaus B (2017), "Educational Status of Muslim Women in India: An overview", *IOSR, journal of humanities and social sciences*, vol-22, Issue-6, e-ISSN: 2279-0837, p-ISSN:2279-0845.

Fredrikson (2004), "Quality Education: The Teacher's Key Role", working paper, retrieved fromhttps://www.basicknowledge101.com/pdf/literacy/Quality%20Education%20 and%20the %20Key%20Role%20of%20Teachers.pdf on 15/04/2019

G

Galloway S (2014) "The Impact of Islam as a Religion and Muslim women on Gender Equality: A Phenomenological Research Study", Ph.D. dissertation submitted to Graduate school of Humanities and Social Sciences, of Nova South Eastern University accessed from https://nsuworks.nova.edu/cgi/viewcontent.cgi?article=1013&context=shssdcaretdon 30/12/2020

Gillies D, (2015), "Human Capital Theory in Education", Encyclopedia of EducationalPhilosophy and Theory", *Springer Science, Business Media* Singapore,

Glick, P. & Sahn, D.E. (2000). Schooling of girls and boys in a West African country:the

effects of parental education, income, and household structure. Economics of EducationReview, 19, 63–87.

Gorham & Diane M. Millette (1997), "A comparative analysis of teacher and student perceptions of sources of motivation and demotivation in college classes", Communication Education,46:4,245-261, DOI:10.1080/03634529709379099

Gouda et, al (2013), "Government Verses Private Schools in India, An assessment ofphysical infrastructure, schooling cost and performance", *International journal of Sociology and social policy*, Vol-33, No-11, accessed from

https://www.emerald.com/insight/content/doi/10.1108/IJSSP-12-2012- 0105/full/html?skipTracking=true on 7/1/2021.

Giri (2014), "A Comparative study on the Academic Achievement of Secondary level students of Joint and Nuclear families in relation to their Values and Adjustment", a synopsis submitted to Gulf Medical University.

Grisay, A., & Mahlck, L. (1991). The quality of education in developing countries: A review of some research studies and policy documents. Paris: International institute of education and planning.

Gunawan I, et, al (2017), "Community Participation in Improving Educational Quality",

2nd International Conference on Educational Management and Administration.

H

Habib et, al (2019), "Impact of Education and Employment on Women Empowerment". *European Online Journal of Natural and Social Sciences*; Vol.8, No 3 (s) ISSN 1805-3602

Haque et, al (2020), "Women's Participation in Education and Politics: Evidence from selected OIC countries" *Journal of Social and Political Sciences*, Vol.3, No.3, 776- 788, accessed from:https://www.asianinstituteofresearch.org on 7/1/2021.

Hoque, M.J. (2016), "Muslim Education in Murshidabad District of West Bengal: Problems and Solutions", *International Journal of Humanities &Social Science Studies,* Vol-2, Issue VI, PageNo.268-272. Retrieved from https://www.ijhsss.com/ on 12/04/2019.

Huisman J. and Smits, J (2009) "Keeping children in school: Household and district-leveldeterminants of school dropout in 363 districts of 30 developing countries.' NICE Working Paper 09-105, Nijmegen: Radboud University.

Hussain (2018), "Educational status of Muslim women in India: Issues and challenges",Scholars *journal of Arts, Humanities and Social Sciences*, ISSN:2347-5374 (print) ISSN:2347-9493 (online), accessed from https://www.researchgate.net/publication/330535000_Educational_Status_of Muslim_Women_in_India_Issues_and_Challenges on 27/12/2020

I

Imtiyaz (2017), "Women Empowerment with special reference to Indian Women, *International journal for studies on children, women, Elderly and Disabled,* Vol-1, ISSN-0128-309X.from

https://www.researchgate.net/publication/320755725_WOMEN_EMPOWERMENT_WITH_SPECIAL_REFERENCE_TO_INDIAN_MUSLIMS on7/1/2021.

J

Jain R and Kabra M (2015) "Teacher Incentives: Evidence from school in Delhi",

Report of center for civil society. Accessed from

https://ccs.in/sites/default/files/research/research-teacher-incentives.pdf on

1/1/2021.

K

Kapur R (2018), "Factors Influencing the Student's Academic Performance in Secondary Schools in India".

Kaur (2011) studied, " A study of academic achievement of school students having illiterateand literate parents, *Journal of Social Science Research*, vol- 1,1retrieved from https://www.researchgate.net/publication/331085189_A_Study_of_Academic

_Achievement_of_School_Students_having_illiterate_and_literate_parents on 2/1/2020.

Kaur and Kaur (2012), "Literacy rates among major religious groups: A geographical perspective", Abstract of Sikh Studies,544, 40-58.

Khalid, W. (2012, April 28). Lack of education is adversely affecting girls. Pakistan Today. Retrieved from https://www.pakistantoday.com.pk/2012/04/28/lack-of-education-is- adversely-affectinggirls/ on 11/11/2020

Khan S (2016) Islam and girl's education: Obligatory of Forbidden", cultural and religiousstudies, vol-4, 6, 339-345, accessed from https://www.researchgate.net/publication/306340964_Islam_and_Girls'_Educ ation_ObligatoryorForbidden on 28/12/2020

Kumari M and Tiwari M, (2012), "Women Education as an Indispensable objective for society and its development in India", *Journal of Advances and scholarly researches in allied education*, Vol-IV, Issue-VII, July, ISSN:2230-7540.

Kundu and Chakraborty (2012), "An Empirical analysis of women Empowerment withinMuslim community in Murshidabad district of West Bengal", *Research on Humanities and Social Sciences,* Vol- N0-6, accessed from https://core.ac.uk/download/pdf/234672987.pdf on 7/1/2021.

Kusumaningrum et, al (2017), "Community Participation in Improving Educational Quality", *Advances in Economics Business and Management Research, Vol 45, Atlantis Press*

L

Lawrence and Hanitha (2017), "A Study on Teachers' Motivational Strategy and Academic Achievement of Higher Secondary Students", AMIER journal

, ISSN 2278-5655, from https://files.eric.ed.gov/fulltext/ED582378.pdf on 7/1/2021.

Lee (2013) "Professional development and Teacher's perception of Efficacy and Inclusion,thesis submitted to School of Graduate studies, East Tennesse State University, accessedfromhttps://core.ac.uk/download/pdf/214067641.pdf on 1/1/2021.

Leung, M. C. M., & Zhang, J. (2008). Gender preference, biased sex ratio, and parental investments in children in single-child households. Review of Economics of the Household 6(2) 91–110.

M

Mabood H. A (1993), "A Study of Attitudes of Teachers and Parents of Azamgarh districttowards Muslim Girl's Education", Jamia Milia Islamia, (Un-published M. ed dissertation)

Mahmood S and Khatoon T, (2011), "Influence of School and Students Factors on Mathematics Achievement", Indian Educational Review- Half yearly journal of Educational Research, vol49, 2

Mancha S and Ahmad A, (2016), " Co- Curricular activities and its effect on Social Skills" in International conference on Education and Regional Development (ICERD) titled, "Cross Cultural education for Sustainable Regional Development" retrieved from https://www.academia.edu/33777339/CO_CURRICULAR_ ACTIVITIES_A ND_ITS_EFFECT_ON_SOCIAL_SKILLS on 27/11/2020

Mangipudy, R., & Venkata, S. (2010). The impact of eliminating extraneous sound and light on students' achievement: An empirical study. Florida, Florida International University, retrieved from https://digitalcommons.fiu.edu/cgi/viewcontent.cgi?article=1 333&context=et d on 30/12/2020.

Mansory, A. (2007), Drop out Study in Basic Education Level of Schools in Afghanistan, Kabul: Swedish committee for Afghanistan. www.nzdl.org/gsdlmod

Mcclendon, D., Hackett, C., Potančoková, M., Stonawski, M., & Skirbekk, V. (2018). Women's Education in the Muslim World. Population and Development Review, 00(0), 1–32. https://doi.org/10.1111/padr.12142

Memo, G.R. Muhammad, F.J &Muhammad, A.K. (2010), "Impact of parental socioeconomic status on students' educational achievement at secondary schools of district Malir, Karachi, Middle East journal of scientific research, Vol. 6. No.6.

Retrieved from

https://www.semanticscholar.org/paper/Impact-of- Parental-Socio-Economic-Status-on-at-of-Joubish-Khurram/f00da1f50600e59858cf90f6d80758149f7d66d8 on 28/11/2020

Michaelowa, K, (2002), "Teacher Job Satisfaction, Student Achievement and the Cost of Primary Education in Francophone Sub- Saharan Africa", HWWA Discussion Paper, Humberg Institute of International Economics.

Mishra B (2010), "Community participation in Quality education", retrieved from https://www.scribd.com/document/22161886/Community-Participation- in-Quality-Education on 25/4/19.

Moneva, Rozado and Sollano (2019) "Parents Occupation and Students' Self-esteem, International journal of Research – Granthalay, vol-7, issue-12, from http://granthaalayah.com/Articles/Vol7Iss12/31_IJRG19_A12_2921.pdfon 8/1/2021.

Muhammed A and Akanle, O (2008), "Socio-Economic Factors Influencing Students Academic Performance in Nigeria Some Explanation from a Local Survey," Sociology and Social work community. Free online library.

Musangu M, (2017) "Parental Socio-economic Status and Academic Performance of Secondary School Students in the Western Province of Republic of Zambia", Working Paper, University of Malaya, DOI: 10.13140/RG.2.2.27743.15520

Muthoni (2013), "Relationship Between Family Background and Academic Performance Of Secondary Schools Students: A Case of Siakago Division, Mbeere North District, Kenya, thesis submitted to University of Nairobi, accessed from http://erepository.uonbi.ac.ke/bitstream/handle/11295/59451/Kamau_Academic%20per formance.pdf?sequence=3 on 8/1/2021.

Mylliemngap (2011) studied "A Study of Infrastructural Facilities of Secondary Schools inShillong Town", dissertation submitted to Department of Education, North Eastern Hill University, Shillong accessed from https://shodhganga.inflibnet.ac.in/handle/10603/169847 on 30/12/2020.

N

Narwana (2015) studied "A global approach to school education and local reality: A case study of community participation in Haryana, Policy Futures in Education 2015, Vol. 13(2) 219–233, accessed from https://journals.sagepub.com/doi/pdf/10.1177/1478210314568242 on2/1/2021

Nasreen (2013), "Education of Muslim women- a journey from past to present", *International journal of Management and Social Sciences,* vol-2 , 1,ISSN:2319-4421,retrieved on 27/12/2020 from
https://www.academia.edu/5373294/EDUCATION_OF_MUSLIM_WOME
N_A_JOURNEY_FROM_PAST_TO_PRESENT

Nepal B (2016), "Relationship Among School's Infrastructure Facilities, LearningEnvironment and Student's Outcome, *International journal of Research for social sciences and humanities in research,* vol- 2 (5), retrieved from

https://www.researchgate.net/publication/326539338_RELATIONSHIP_AMONG_SC
HOOL'S_INFRASTRUCTURE_FACILITIES_LEARNING_ENVIRONMENT_AND

_STUDENT'S_OUTCOME on 30/12/2020

Nirmala K and Selvi P (2012), "Promoting smart Schools with Community Participation- An experimental Study at the Grassroots in India", a dissertation submitted to Mother Teressa Women's University, Retrieved from

https://shodhganga.inflibnet.ac.in/handle/10603/263581

Nishimura M (2017), "Community Participation in School Management in Developing Countries", retrieved from https://doi.org/10.1093/acrefore/9780190264093.013.64 on 6/12/2020

Noor (2016), "Challenges of Islamic Education in Muslim World: Historical, Political and Socio- cultural Perspective, *Qudus international journal of Islamic studies, (4)*, (1) pp- 82-105.

Noorain (2018), "Islam on Women Education"- A Societal Perspective, Ph. D thesis submitted to Department of Education, University of Lucknow, accessed from https://shodhganga.inflibnet.ac.in/handle/10603/240011 on 1/1/2021.

O

Ogunshola, F., &Adewale, A.M. (2012). The Effects of Parental Socio- Economic Status onAcademic Performance of Students in Selected Schools in EduLga of Kwara State Nigeria. *International Journal of Academic Research in Business and Social Sciences,* 2(7), 2222-6990

Ogunsola, Osuolale, & Ojo (2014), " Parental and related factors affecting StudentsAcademic Achievement in Oyo state , Nigeria", World Academy of Science,Engineering and Technology, *International Journal of Social, Education, Economicsand Management Engineering* Vol:8, No:9, https://www.researchgate.net/publiction/328858106_Parental _and_related_factors_affe cting_Students_Academic_Achievement_in_Oyo_State_Nige ria on 4/12/2020 on7/1/2021.

Ononuga, F (2005), "Relationship between Socio- Economic Status and AcademicAchievement in Economics", Unpublished B. Ed Project, University of Ibadan

P

Pande (2006), "Muslim Women and girls education: A Case study from Hyderabad", Journal of Indian Education, Volume XXXII, 1

Parveen (2009-10), "Exclusion of Muslim girls from schools: A participatory analysis in the district of Rampur"- A study supported by Child Rights and You.

Pratap S (2015), Empowerment of Muslim Women, Indian Journal of Research, Vol-4,10,retrieved from https://www.researchgate.net/publication/283539413_Empowerment_of_Muslim_Women/link/563dbf9308aec6f17dd8c601/download on 28/12/2020

Preetham (2008), "Co-Curricular activities, attitudes and participation of Secondary schoolstudents", Thesis submitted to Acharya Nagarjuna University accessed from http://shodhganga.inflibnet.ac.in:8080/jspui/handle/10603/127111 on 1/1/2021

Prema (2016), studied "Parental Involvement in Relation with Academic Achievement of Progeny, *Indian journal of Applied Research*", Volume: 6, Issue: 5, ISSN - 2249-555X

Q

Qadri (2018) studied, "Parental Educational Status and Academic Achievement of Students, IJCRT, Volume 6, Issue 1, ISSN: 2320-2882

R

Rabiya (2017), "Psychological Wellbeing, Study Involvement and Academic Environment of Government and Private Secondary School Students – A Comparative Study"- thesis submitted to school of education, Central University of Kashmir retrieved from https://shodhganga.inflibnet.ac.in/handle/10603/222956 on 8/1/2021.

Rajitha (2011) undertook a study on, "Study on the Influence of Parental Education and Occupation on the Achievement Motivation of adolescents, *International journal of Science and Research,* Vol-5 issue 10, ISSN (Online): 2319-7064, retrieved from https://www.ijsr.net/archive/v5i10/ART20162379.pdf on 2/1/2020.

Reid, K., Hopkins, D., & Holly, P. (1987), "Towards the Effective School". Oxford: BasilRetrieved from https://www.econstor.eu/bitstream/10419/19349/1/188.pdf on 15/04/2019. Retrieved from https://www.researchgate.net/publication/324819919_Factors _Influencing_the_Student s_Aca demic_Performance_in_Secondary_Schools_in_India on18/04/2019

Roja, Sasikumar and Fathima (2013), " A study on Emotional maturity and Self Conceptat Higher Educational level, Research in psychology and Behavioral Sciences, Vol-1 , 5 accessed fromhttps://www.researchgate.net/publication/329773300_A _Study_on_Emotiona l_Maturity_and_Self_Concept_at_Higher_Secondary_Level on 1/1/2021.

S

Saba et, al (2017), "Education as a powerful weapon for empowering Muslim women in West Bengal, *International Journal of Advanced Educational Research",* Vol-2 Issue-3. ISSN: 2455-6157.

Saha S (2020), "Educational Status of Muslim Women in West Bengal: A case Study of Chhapra Block of Nadia

District, *NSOU – open Journal*, Vol-3,1 accessed from https://www.researchgate.net/publication/342464810_Educational_Status_ofMuslim_Women_in_West_Bengal_A_Case_Study_of_Chapra_Block_in_Nadia_District on 29/12/2020

Saifullah and Mehmood, (2011) On, "Effects of Socioeconomic Status on Students Achievement, *International Journal of Social Sciences and Education,* Vol-1, Issue- 2,retrieved fromhttps://www.ijsse.com/sites/default/files/issues/2011/v1i2/p3/Paper.pdfon 28/11/2020

Saila T.S and Chamudeshwari S (2014), "Development of Socio- EconomicBackgroundScale", *International Journal of Current Research and Academic* Review, Vol-12, Page78-83 Retrieved on 24/4/2019 from http://www.ijcrar.com/vol12/T.%20Sahaya%20Saila%20and%20S.%20Cha mundeswari.pdf

Salam N (2019), ""Education and Empowerment of Muslim Women in the district of Murshidabad: West Bengal", IMPACT : *International Journal of Research in Humanities* , Arts and Literature, Vol-7, 3, ISSN (P): 2347-4564;ISSN (E): 2321-8878, accessed from http://oaji.net/articles/2019/488-1555412985.pdf on 27/12/2020

Sanders and Lewis (2005), "Building Bridges Towards Excellence: CommunityInvolvement in High Schools", The High School Journal, Vol-88 No-3, University ofNorth Carolina Press, retrieved from

https://www.researchgate.net/profile/Mavis_Sanders/publication/236807841_Building_ Bridges_Toward_Excellence_Community_Involvement_in_ High_ Schools/links/578cfcac08ae254b1d on 7/12/2020.

Schneider, M. (2002). Do School Facilities Affect Academic Outcomes? Washington, DC:National Clearinghouse for

Educational Facilities. Retrieved on March 1, 2019, from http://www.edfacilities.org/pubs/outcomes

Sekhar, Reddy and Nagarjuna (2014) studied, "A Study of Teacher's Motivation of Teachers in Relation to Certain Factors, *Indian journal of Applied Research,* vol-4, Issue-4 , ISSN: 2249-555X, derived fromhttps://www.worldwidejournals.com/indian- journal-of-applied-research-(IJAR)/recent_issues_pdf/2014/April/April_2014_13963673 95_0f81f_38.pdfon7/1/2021.

Shah et, al (2011), conducted a study on "A Study on Status of empowerment of Women inJamnagar district, *National Journal of community medicines*, vol- 2, Issue-3 from http://njcmindia.org/uploads/2-3_423-428.pdf on 7/1/2021.

Shahidul S and Karim S, (2015), "Factors Contributing to School Dropout Among the Girls: A Review of Literature", *European journal of research and reflection in educational sciences,* Vol-3, N0-2, ISSN: 2056-5852

Sharma Pratima Devi (2011), "Influence of the Women teacher in the Education of the Women (Girl Child) in the Rural and Minority Area of Nagaon District', *Journal of Social Sciences*, Volume 1, No. 3, pp 43-52.

Sharma R, Goswami V, Gupta P (2016), "Social Skills: Their Impact on Academic Achievement and Other Aspects of Life", International journal for and innovative research in Multidisciplinary field, Vol-2 Issue-7, ISSN: 2455-0620. Retrieved from https://www.ijirmf.com/wp-content/uploads/2016/11/201607049.pdf on 27/11/2020

Sharma T.N (2008), "Structure and Mechanism of Community Participation in School Management, *Journal of education and Research,* 1, 72-85, retrieved from https://kusoed.edu.np/journal/index.php/je/article/view/78 on 6/12/2020.

Shazia (2016), "Health and Empowerment: A Sociological Study of Women in AligarhCity, Ph. D thesis submitted to Department of Sociology, Aligarh Muslim University, retrieved fromhttps://core.ac.uk/download/pdf/144527433.pdf on 6/1/2021.

Shazli T and Asma S (2015), "Educational Vision of Muslims in India: Problems and Concerns", *International Journal of Humanities and Social Science Invention* ISSN (Online): 2319 – 7722, ISSN (Print): 2319 – 7714, Vol-4, Issue-3.

Shovan, G. & Susmita, S. (2012). Direct and opportunity costs of schooling a girl child: Acase study of puncha block of purulia District, West Bengal, India. *International Journal of Current Research*, (4)12, 376-381

Singh (2015), "Empowerment of Muslim Women", Indian Journal of Research, Vol-4, 10, accessed from

https://www.researchgate.net/publication/283539413_Empowerment_of_Muslim_Women on 29/12/2020

Singh P and Chaudhary G (2015), "Impact of Socio-economic status on academic achievement of school students", *International Journal of Applied Research*, Vol-1, (4), ISSN Print: 2394-7500 ISSN Online: 2394-5869, accessed from https://www.allresearchjournal.com/archives/2015/vol1issue4/PartE/28. 1.pdf on 1/1/2021.

Singh, A. (2017). Effect of Co-Curricular Activities on Academic Achievement of Students.IRA *International Journal of Education and Multidisciplinary Studies* (ISSN 2455- 2526), 6(3), 241-254.

Sirait S (2016), "Does Teacher Quality Affect Student Achievement? An Empirical Study in Indonesia. *journal of*

Education and Practice, Vol-7, 27, ISSN:2222-1735, (print), 2222-288X (online), retrieved from https://files.eric.ed.gov/fulltext/EJ1115867.pdf on 31/12/2020.

Sirin, S.R., (2005), "Socioeconomic Status and Academic Achievement: A Meta Analytic Review of Research", *Review of EducationalResearch*.75(3),417– 453.

Smits, Mulder & Hooimeijer, (2003), "Migration of couples with non-employed andemployed wives in the Netherlands-The changing effects of the partner's characteristics", *Journal of Ethnic and Migration Studies,* retrieved from https://www.researchgate.net/publication/238398565_Migration_of_couples_with_non-employed_and_employed_wives_in_the_Netherlands_The_changing_effects_of_the_partners_'_characteristics on 28/11/2020

Swart, A. (1999), "Evaluation of the assessment strategy for admission at Pretoria University"., Retrieved on 24/4/19,from http://hagar.up.ac.za/catts/learner/andres/assess.html

T

Taiguara et., al (2020), "A Stakeholder Theory Approach to creating value in higher education institutions" Retrieved fromhttps://www.emerald.com/insight/publication/issn/0888-045X on 5/11/2020 DOI 10.1108/BL-03-2020-0021 on 30/10/2020

Tallat R (2010), "Development of Social Skills among Children at ElementaryLevel",

Bulletin of Education and Research, Vol- 32, No-1.

Talukdar (2015), "Education and Empowerment of Muslim Women in West Bengal", Ph. D thesis submitted to

Department of Education, University of Kalyani. http://shodhganga.inflibnet.ac.in:8080/jspui/handle/10603/103333 on 30/12/2020

U

Ummer and Shanmugam (2017), "A Study on Infrastructural Facilities in Schools of Kulgam District (J&K), *BRDU- International journal of multidisciplinary research,* Vol-2, Issue- 3, from http://ijmdr.in/data/documents/MARCH_PAPER-3.PDF on 7/1/2021.

V

Vayaliparampil (2012). "Stakeholders Perception of the Sarva Shiksha AbhiyanEffectiveness in increasing school enrolment in India, Dissertation submitted to

Pennsylvania state university, retrieved from https://etda.libraries.psu.edu/catalog/16371 on 9/1/2021.

Vellymallay (2011), "A Study of the relationship between Indian parents educational leveland their involvement in their children's education", Kajiyan Malaysia, vol-29, no-2 from http://web.usm.my/km/29(2)2011/Art3_KM29- 2.pdf on 8/1/2021.

Vijayakalshmi and Muniappan (2016), "Parental Involvement and achievement of schoolstudents, *The international journal of Indian Psychology*, Volume 3, Issue 4, ISSN 2348-5396 (e) | ISSN: 2349-3429 (p) retrieved from https://ijip.in/wpcontent/uploads/ArticlesPDF/article_d0c47186067a1d94a71 9R91ae516d7f3a.pdf on 2/1/2021.

W

Walter (2018), A study on "Influence of Parental Occupation and Parental income on students' Academic performance in Public Day Secondary Schools", *World Journal of Innovative research,* Volume-5, Issue-6, ISSN:2454-8236,retrieved from https://www.wjir.org/download_data/WJIR0506018.pdf on 2/1/2021

Waseem S and Ahmad A (2012), "Muslim omen Education and Empowerment in rural Aligarh", *International journal of scientific and research publications, vol-2.* 4 ISSN- 2250-3153 accessed from http://www.ijsrp.org/research_paper_apr2012/ijsrp-apr-2012-41.pdf on27/12/2020

Z

Zehri, Chokri & Abdelbaki, Asma (2013), "Does adoption of international accounting standards promote economic growth in developing countries? ",*International Open Journal of Economics,* Vol. 1, No. 1, July, p.01 retrieved from https://pdfs.semanticscholar.org/5a6a/ff48b9cac5f7befbea8fe32703e44528c338.pdf on 28/11/2020

Zellman & Waterman, (1998) on "Understanding the Impact of Parent School Involvement on Children's Educational Outcome", *the Journal of Educational Research,* Vol. 91, No. 6 (Jul. - Aug., 1998), Taylor and Francis, retrieved from https://www.jstor.org/stable/27542180?seq=1 on 29/11/2020.

Zengenene, M., & Susanti, E. (2019). Violence against women and girls in Harare, Zimbabwe. *Journal of International Women's studies,* 20 (9), 83-93

Zigarelli MA (1996), "An empirical test of conclusions from effective schools", Journalof Educational Research, 90(2): 103-111

Publications by National and International bodies and web references

An NEA Policy brief on "Parent, Family, Community Involvement in Education" by NEAEducation Policy and Practice Department, Centre for great public school, Washington. Retrieved from http://www.nea.org/assets/docs/PB11_ParentInvolvement08.pdf on 25/4/19. Ofsted –(Office for Standards in Education)- An Annual Report of Her Majesty's chief Inspector of Schools. Retrieved from https://assets.publishing.service.gov.uk/government/uploads/system/uploads/ attachment data/file/265506/129.pdf on 29/11/2020

United Nations (UN) General Assembly. (1948). Universal declaration of human rights (217 [III] A – Article 26). Paris, France: Author. Retrieved from http://www.un.org/en/universaldeclaration-human-rights/ on 8/8/2020

United Nations (UN) General Assembly. (1979). Convention on the elimination of all formsof discrimination against women (Session 34, Resolution 180). New York, NY:

United Nations (UN) General Assembly. (1989). Convention on the rights of the child (Session 44, Resolution 25). Retrieved from http://www.ohchr.org/EN/ProfessionalInterest/Pages/CRC.aspx on 8/8/2020

United Nations Educational, Scientific, and Cultural Organization (UNESCO). (2013). Girls'education: The Facts Retrieved from

http://en.unesco.org/gem- report/sites/gemreport/files/girls-factsheet-en.pdf

United Nations Educational, Scientific, and Cultural Organization (UNESCO). (2013). Girl'sand women's right to education: overview of the measures supporting the right to education for girls and women reported on by member states.

United Nations Educational, Scientific, and Cultural Organization (UNESCO). (2000a). Conference report: Asia-Pacific conference on education for all 2000 assessment. Bangkok, Thailand: Author.

United Nations Educational, Scientific, and Cultural Organization (UNESCO). (2000b). TheDakar framework for action: Education for all. Paris, France: Author.

https://www.india.gov.in/spotlight/rashtriya-madhyamik-shiksha-abhiyan#tab=tab-

http://minorityaffairs.gov.in/en/schemesperformance/maulana-azad-national- fellowship-minority-students-scheme

http://www.minorityaffairs.gov.in/reports/sachar-committee-report

Sachar Committee Report (2006). Social Economic and Educational Status of Muslim Community in India. New Delhi: Cabinet Secretariat, Government of India.

https://www.education.gov.in/en/aishe-report-2018-19
https://censusindia.gov.in/2011census/population_enumeration.html

www.ingramcontent.com/pod-product-compliance
Lightning Source LLC
LaVergne TN
LVHW061545070526
838199LV00077B/6910